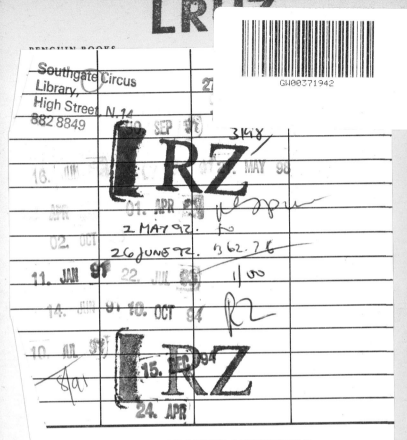

Gay Search

The Last Taboo

Sexual Abuse of Children

PENGUIN BOOKS

PENGUIN BOOKS

Published by the Penguin Group
27 Wrights Lane, London w8 5tz, England
Viking Penguin Inc., 40 West 23rd Street, New York, New York 10010, USA
Penguin Books Australia Ltd, Ringwood, Victoria, Australia
Penguin Books Canada Ltd, 2801 John Street, Markham, Ontario, Canada l3r 1b4
Penguin Books (NZ) Ltd, 182–190 Wairau Road, Auckland 10, New Zealand

Penguin Books Ltd, Registered Offices: Harmondsworth, Middlesex, England

First published 1988
10 9 8 7 6 5 4 3 2 1

The characters portrayed in this book are real and the events described all took place,
but I have used fictional names and omitted descriptive details in places where I have
felt that this would protect privacy

Made and printed in Great Britain by
Richard Clay Ltd, Bungay, Suffolk

Filmset in 10 on 12pt Monophoto Bembo

Contents

Acknowledgements

I would like to thank the many people working in the field of child sexual abuse and quoted in this book who so generously gave me the benefit of their experience and wisdom. I would also like to thank Sarah Caplin and Catherine Boyd of the BBC's Childwatch team for their help and encouragement in the early stages.

Above all, my thanks are due to the many men and women – victims, parents, abusers – who shared their often still painful memories with me in the hope that by so doing they might help someone else in the same situation.

Foreword

by Richard Johnson, Director, Incest Crisis Line

Over the past ten or fifteen years there has been an upsurge of material written about the subject of child sexual abuse. Many of the books produced seemed only to perpetuate all the myths and pre-conceived ideas that abound on this subject; not many of them, if indeed any, took into account the feelings of readers who, because they themselves had been abused, were looking for an understanding approach to the problems they were experiencing.

The perpetuation of myths like: 'All abusers were abused as children'; 'All mothers must know'; 'She must have enjoyed it to let it go on for so long'; 'Kids fantasize'; 'It only happens in working-class or ethnic minority families'; 'Abused children will grow up to abuse their own kids', and so on, only serve to make the lot of those of us who were abused harder to deal with.

This book begins to address these and many other misconceptions. The author doesn't presume to provide answers, and indeed she is well aware that those answers are not yet available, but instead she questions the theories and outmoded concepts that still prevail.

Incest and child sexual abuse are major problems in this and most other societies on earth. The proper education of people working with these problems is of paramount importance; a good and sensitive approach at the time of disclosure can save a lifetime of pain and anguish for abused children.

Publications that question instead of providing uninformed and half-hearted attempts at answers must be good. No one person is a true expert in this field. We are all still learning and I think this book makes that point quite succinctly.

It also successfully emphasizes the need for inter-agency coopera-tion. With each agency having its own systems and procedures, which in the main, work against one another, a coming together of all those agencies, both voluntary and statutory, can only serve to

benefit the children and families that are being torn apart by disclosures of sexual abuse.

I hope this book will be the first in a long line of honest
portrayals of the problem, because, God knows, we have been in
need of them for a long time.

Richard A. Johnson
Director and Senior Counsellor,
Incest Crisis Line

Introduction: Cleveland 1987

In July 1987, Cleveland, in the north-east of England, hit the headlines in a big way. At the beginning of the month the press discovered that, in the previous six months, over 100 children had been removed from their parents on Place of Safety orders, at the request of the social services department and as a result of diagnoses of sexual abuse by two paediatricians at Middlesbrough General Hospital, Dr Marietta Higgs and Dr Geoffrey Wyatt. The resulting storm of controversy raged throughout the rest of the year, culminating in the longest judicial inquiry ever held. Lord Justice Elizabeth Butler-Sloss presided over the inquiry, which lasted 74 days, cost £4 million and heard evidence from 136 witnesses. Her 700-page report was published in July 1988 (see Chapter 8).

Obviously Cleveland is no Sodom and Gomorrah, so why was this apparent epidemic of child sexual abuse suddenly sweeping through its population? Or was the explanation that people who had been trained in what to look for were now recognizing something that had been there all along?

In June 1986, Dr Higgs, a well-respected paediatrician with an interest in child abuse then working in Newcastle, attended a two-day course given by the Leeds paediatricians Drs Hobbs and Wynne explaining their diagnostic techniques, including the now notorious reflex anal dilatation (RAD), which are described in Chapter 1. The following month, using those techniques, she examined a five-year-old girl and diagnosed sexual abuse.

In January 1987, Dr Higgs was appointed consultant paediatrician at Middlesbrough General Hospital. In the first six months she diagnosed 78 cases of child sexual abuse out of 102 referred to her, though in only 8 of them was RAD the only physical symptom. According to the judge in one court case, during a 28-day period in May and June Dr Higgs had found 52 cases of sexual abuse out of 71 children examined. Not only those children but their brothers and sisters, also thought to be at risk of abuse, were removed from home under Place of Safety orders issued by magistrates. Although Cleveland social services had given child abuse top priority in the light of Louis Blom-Cooper's report on the Jasmine Beckford affair and had appointed a specialist, Sue Richardson, they found they simply didn't have the resources to cope with the numbers of children suddenly being taken into care. When the social services department ran out of foster parents, some were put into hospital wards that were already overcrowded with sick children.

There were howls of outrage from the parents concerned – both innocent and guilty alike. (One of the major problems in investigating child sexual abuse is denial. Few abusers will admit – even to themselves – what they have done.) The local MP, Stuart Bell, took up the parents' cause, accusing the social services department of 'empire-building', demanding the suspension of Drs Higgs and Wyatt, even warning parents of the risks involved in taking their children to Middlesbrough General for any reason.

I am not for one moment minimizing the nightmare of parents who were wrongly accused, and the harm done to children who were taken into care and kept from their families for eighteen months and more. That was appalling and should never have happened. But suddenly the focus of Cleveland had become the territorial disputes between the different professions, and the clash between professionals' and parents' rights. In the process the children, some of whom had undoubtedly been sexually abused, were largely forgotten.

When the row broke nationally, the tabloid press which only months before had vilified social workers for their failure to remove children from physically abusing parents, was vilifying them still more strongly for removing children from parents suspected of sexual abuse. The hysteria and denial that surrounded Cleveland demonstrated very clearly our unwillingness to accept the likely scale of the problem. To do so means accepting that at least one child in our own children's class at school has probably been or is being sexually abused. It also means that the people who abuse children sexually are not a monstrous aberration. They're likely to be people we know, people like us. It means that sexual abuse isn't an epidemic, a sudden outbreak of abnormal behaviour. It means that it is, and has long been, endemic in this society, woven closely into its fabric.

Although the very name of Cleveland has become synonymous with child sexual abuse and the responses to it, the events there happened at a time when awareness of the problem was already growing. Esther Rantzen's first BBC TV 'Childwatch' programme in 1986, for example, had revealed that child sexual abuse was widespread, and ChildLine, the free telephone line for all abused children, had been set up as a result.

Since Cleveland, though, it has been almost impossible to open a newspaper without reading something about child sexual abuse – a court case, a government initiative, a change in the law. There have been many magazine articles, and radio and television programmes, both documentaries and drama. Some of the coverage has been excellent, but overall it has created more heat than light. Sometimes you would get the impression that every child in the country was either being abused or was in very real danger of being so. At other times, you might be led to believe that the whole furore was simply an outbreak of hysteria whipped up by a few zealots, and that it actually involved a very small number of children.

I, like most parents, was deeply concerned – though, like most ordinary people, I was also confused. Writing this book has been a voyage of discovery for me, trying to sort out fact from fiction, myths from reality, and I can only hope that what I have found will help other people to do the same. It was a depressing experience in many ways. In addition to the sheer size of the problem, and the fact that we as a society really don't yet know how to cope with it, the catalogue of almost inconceivable depravity – the three-year-old girl with gonorrhoea, the eleven-year-old boy anally raped by his mother with the handle of a toy dagger, the eight-year-old hired out for sex by her father – was sometimes numbing. But there were a few reasons for optimism too. There is rapidly growing knowledge and sensitivity among professionals working in the field and some excellent work is being done, though nothing like enough. Above all, there is the courage and strength of some victims who, in spite of appalling childhood experiences, are determined to survive them and make something of their lives. We can only hope that, as more help gradually becomes available, many more severely damaged people will be able to do the same.

AUTHOR'S NOTE. Because we have no third person singular pronouns in the English language we can apply to both sexes, for convenience I have referred to victims and abusers in general terms as 'she' and 'he' respectively since the majority in each group are of that gender.

1 A Modern Epidemic?

Perhaps the most useful point at which to start any exploration of child sexual abuse would be with a definition of exactly what it is. There have been many definitions, and one of the simplest and most widely accepted is that quoted by Ruth and Henry Kempe, the American paediatricians who first described the 'battered baby syndrome' in the 1960s:

> Sexual abuse is the involvement of dependent, developmentally immature children or adolescents in sexual activities they do not truly comprehend, to which they are unable to give informed consent or that violate the sexual taboos of family roles.

Another more complicated but also more comprehensive definition is that laid down by the Standing Committee on Sexually Abused Children, a charitable organization founded in 1983:

> Any child below the age of consent may be deemed to have been sexually abused when a sexually mature person has, by design or neglect of their usual societal or specific responsibilities in relation to the child, engaged or permitted the engagement of that child in any activity of a sexual nature which is intended to lead to the sexual gratification of the sexually mature person. This definition pertains whether or not this activity involves explicit coercion by any means, whether or not it involves genital or physical contact, whether or not initiated by the child, and whether or not there is discernible harmful outcome in the short term.

It is a legalistic mouthful, but it does cover every possible kind of abuse, from taking pornographic photographs and indecent exposure, through procuring children for other adults or failing to protect them from sexually predatory adults, to taking advantage of a child who, as a result of previous sexual abuse, is sexually provocative; in fact every conceivable – and inconceivable – kind of sexual activity. In defining abuse, it also stresses the importance of the abuser's intentions. Any activity which in itself might be harmless becomes abusive if it is done with the sole purpose of giving the abuser sexual gratification. One man, for example, who served two years for incest and indecent assault, liked being tickled by twelve- and thirteen-year-old girls. What made it abusive was that it aroused him sexually.

The kind of activities covered by the term 'child sexual abuse' range from indecent exposure ('flashing'), talking obscenely to a child either in person or on the telephone, looking at their naked bodies, photographing them, fondling their genitals, mutual masturbation, and oral, anal or vaginal sex. Some people would exclude indecent exposure or talking obscenely, and only count activities that involve physical contact. Others think that only penetration counts as 'real' child sexual abuse.

Anne Bannister, who runs the NSPCC and Greater Manchester Authorities Child Sexual Abuse Unit, believes we all make our own rules. 'Some people throw up their hands in horror at someone abusing a seven-year-old girl. Some of them are less horrified if it's someone else's daughter rather than their own. Other people say, "Oral sex? My goodness, that's terrible!", but think that vaginal intercourse is OK. Still others think that as long as it's everything but vaginal intercourse – oral sex, anal sex, whatever – that's not so bad because at least the hymen isn't broken so she isn't "damaged goods". Or they'll say "Well, if the abuser is the girl's stepbrother, even though he is eight years older than she is and has total power over her, that's not so bad as if it were her father." It's absolute nonsense, of course. There are so many other variables that you can't simply look at the bald facts and estimate the damage done. What looks like very severe abuse might do less damage to one victim than what seems like comparatively "mild" abuse might do to another.'

In the light of all the current concern about the subject, it's also important to know what sexual abuse is *not*. Many parents, fathers especially, are concerned about the dangers of ordinary day-to-day activities, such as cuddling, kissing, bathing and drying their children, being misinterpreted. (It was unfortunate that in a recent television play, based on events in Cleveland, the doctor who diagnosed sexual abuse in a five-year-old girl seemed to see an ulterior motive in the fact that the child's father often bathed and dried her and put cream on her sore bottom.)

The NSPCC was quick to respond to parents' fears. Their booklet, 'Protect Your Child', says it is perfectly natural for parents

> to cuddle, hug, kiss and stroke their children when showing love and affection. All these activities are normal and acceptable and, as we have seen, to deny a child love and affection constitutes neglect. Children can enjoy physical play but if your child feels uncomfortable it is time to stop. It is not normal for any adult to become sexually excited or aroused by their own children.

In other words, if it turns you on, it's wrong.

Other people take the view that it's not quite that simple and straightforward. Anne Bannister, for example, believes that many people have sexual feelings towards children. 'And that's not just guesswork. In training programmes I run and group support work I do, I ask people about it, and those who have really thought about their own sexuality will usually say, "Yes, it's true." It's what they do with those feelings that matters. And the vast majority simply put them away, and that's that. But just having acknowledged that they exist is good.

'People who have them but don't acknowledge them don't necessarily become abusers, but they may well get into abusive behaviour – flicking girls' bras, telling little girls how sexy they look. They, of course, would deny it's abusive. They'd say it was just a bit of fun, but to me it's potentially dangerous because they haven't even recognized their own feelings.'

There are groups and individuals who argue that, provided no force or coercion is used, sexual activities with children are not necessarily abusive. But most of them, though not all, are paedophiles – men who are primarily sexually aroused by children who haven't yet reached puberty – and so the argument has to be seen as special pleading.

However, most people still take the view that any sexual relationship between an adult and a child, even if no force or threat or overt coercion is used, is of its very nature abusive. A child is physically smaller and weaker than an adult, and in every other sense less powerful. Children, by virtue of the fact that they *are* children, are dependent on adults for their very survival. To suggest, as the paedophile lobby and its fellow-travellers do, that a child is able to give consent to a sexual relationship with an adult is to suggest an equality in status and power that simply doesn't exist. At its simplest, children are expected to do what adults tell them to do. They are not, on the whole, brought up to negotiate or to feel free to say no.

As for sexual activity, children simply do not have the experience or the understanding of all its ramifications, or its long-term consequences physically, emotionally or psychologically, to be able to give informed consent. And the argument that such relationships can be 'enriching' because they offer some children the only closeness and affection they get is rather like giving whisky to a baby starved of milk on the grounds that some liquid is better than none at all.

HOW WIDESPREAD IS IT?

The scale of the problem is extremely hard to assess. As I have said, secrecy is a fundamental part of child sexual abuse, and it is impossible to know how widespread it is. Certainly nobody would dispute that the official Home Office statistics are merely the tip of an iceberg. In 1987, for example, there were 511 incest offences recorded by the police in England and Wales (67 more than in the previous year), 831 offences of gross indecency with a child (masturbation of a boy, mutual masturbation, oral sex), an increase of 165 on 1986, and 2,699 offences of unlawful sexual intercourse with a girl under sixteen. Statistics for most other sexual offences, such as rape, buggery and indecent assault, include cases where the victims are over sixteen as well as under (as indeed do reported cases of incest), so there is no way of knowing the exact number of sexual offences against children. Many other cases never even get that far. According to the NSPCC, in 1986 court proceedings were considered in only 30 per cent of cases.

Child sexual abuse cases are notoriously difficult to prosecute. As the law stands, a defendant cannot be convicted on the uncorroborated evidence of a young child. The very nature of child sexual abuse means that there are very rarely witnesses. And since most child abuse does not involve penetration, there are seldom physical signs. Given that many cases don't come to light right away, there is usually no forensic evidence either. Even if there is some corroboration – a child found in a distressed state or showing a number of symptoms associated with abuse – there is always the problem of how good a witness the child will be.

The changes proposed by the new Criminal Justice Bill, which allow a child to give evidence in some Crown Court cases from another room via a video link, may well help in the future. But in the past, the experience of having to appear in court was devastating for many children and they broke down. It was not simply having to face a battery of strangers wearing forbidding costumes in a setting designed to inspire awe, or being cross-examined by one of those strangers in a way that made no concession to the fact that the child was the victim as well as a witness and maybe only nine or ten years old; giving evidence in great detail, only feet away from the abuser who may have threatened the child with the direst consequences if she told, or, just as painful, whom she still loves and for whose current plight she feels wholly responsible, was often unbearable.

Extraordinary though it may seem, it was only on 1 April 1988 that any government department – the DHSS, in fact – started to compile national statistics on child sexual abuse. Although every local authority has had to keep a Child Abuse Register since 1974, it was only in 1987 that they were surveyed by the Association of Directors of Social Services and a national figure produced – 29,666 children, though as not every register records from what type of abuse a child is at risk, there is no separate figure for sexual abuse.

In 1987 the NSPCC had 639 sexually abused children on the twelve Child Abuse Registers it keeps for some local authorities' Area Review Committees, which represents an increase of 21 per cent over the figures for 1986, which in turn represented an increase of 137 per cent over the figures for 1985. The NSPCC reckons that approximately 9 per cent of all the children in England and Wales live in the areas covered by its registers, so by multiplying up, they estimate that some 7,000 children are registered as being at risk of sexual abuse.

Most people agree that these dramatic increases have much more to do with recent publicity, and both public and professional awareness of the problem, than with any sudden rise in abuse itself. But even so, these figures are widely believed to be only a fraction of the real total. In its first year, for example, ChildLine, the confidential telephone line for children in trouble or danger set up after Esther Rantzen's first 'Childwatch' programme on BBC TV, dealt with nearly 6,000 cases of sexual abuse. Although many social work agencies had been opposed to ChildLine on the grounds that they would not be able to cope with a deluge of disclosures, in fact 95 per cent of the callers refuse to give their full names and addresses so that they *can't* be referred to other helping agencies. And while it is clear that some children, having talked to a ChildLine counsellor, have then told an adult who can do something to stop the abuse, the vast majority tell no one and therefore do not appear in any official statistics.

Other very strong evidence for believing that child sexual abuse is far more widespread than official figures suggest comes from retrospective studies, in which adults are asked about their sexual experiences in childhood. An often quoted – and, indeed, often misquoted – MORI poll carried out in 1985 interviewed over 2,000 men and women aged from fifteen upwards, not simply chosen at random but selected as a nationally representative sample. The definition of sexual abuse they were given was any sexual activity in which a sexually mature person involved children for his or her own gratification, and specified 'intercourse, touching, exposing of the sexual organs, showing pornographic material or talking about sexual things in an erotic way'. Ten per cent of the sample – 12 per cent of the women and 8 per cent of the men – said they had such experiences before they reached sixteen, and 77 per cent said they hadn't; the remaining 13 per cent refused to answer.

In his study of 600 women carried out in 1985, Donald West, Emeritus Professor of Criminology at Cambridge University, found that 46 per cent of them had suffered from sexual abuse as defined in similar broad terms to those of the MORI poll, while in the same year another researcher, Ruth Hall, found that 21 per cent of the women in her study had been sexually abused as children, a third of them more than once.

Figures from other English-speaking countries such as Canada, Australia and the USA, which have similar social problems to our own, suggest that our figures may, if anything, be on the low side. The Badgley Committee's Report on Sexual Offences against Children and Youths, commissioned by the Canadian government in 1984, found that 34 per cent of women and about 13 per cent of men had, before they reached the age of eighteen, been 'victims of one or more unwanted sexual acts. These acts include: being exposed to; being sexually threatened; being touched on a sexual part of the body, and attempts to assault or being sexually assaulted'. Diana Russell's study, carried out on a random sample of 913 women in San Francisco in 1983, defined sexual abuse more narrowly, limiting it to experiences that involved physical contact, from fondling to rape. Of the women questioned, 38 per cent had been sexually abused at least once before they were eighteen, while 29 per cent had been abused before their fourteenth birthday. Other reputable studies carried out in the USA have found lower rates. One study based on a national sample of both men and women in 1985 found that 16 per cent and 27 per cent respectively had been sexually abused as children, while David Finkelhor's 1979 study of college students in New England produced figures of 9 per cent and 19 per cent.

Although it is important in terms of public policy to try and get a clear picture of the scale of the problem, there are real dangers in getting too caught up in the numbers game. Attention is focused on whether there are a million children at risk of being sexually abused, as some studies suggest; or whether there are 'only' one or two hundred thousand, as though somehow the lower figure is acceptable. Given the damage we know sexual abuse can do, it is wholly unacceptable for even one child to be abused, never mind one hundred thousand. We don't know for certain what the true figures are, but in a sense that isn't important. What is indisputably true is that child sexual abuse is – and has long been – much more widespread than anyone would have dreamt ten years ago, and that we have a major problem on our hands. As public awareness and professional expertise increase, so do the number of cases uncovered. It almost seems as though the former dictates the pace of the latter. Michele Elliott, founder of Kidscape, the personal safety programme for children, and a pioneer in the field of child sexual abuse prevention, believes that is the case. 'Not so long ago, when I first talked to people in authority about doing preventative work in schools and helping children who are being abused to disclose the fact, the response was "But what if they do disclose? We wouldn't be able to cope!" It's as though they're saying, "Yes, we know you're out there, kids, but please give us a couple of years to sort ourselves out and get our act together!"'

INTERPRETING THE FIGURES

Another problem with all the statistics on child sexual abuse is that people don't read the small print. The fact that one in ten children – or one in six, or one in four – is the victim of sexual abuse is often taken to mean that one child in ten is brutally raped. That simply isn't true. The MORI poll found that in 51 per cent of cases there was no physical contact – the abuse was indecent exposure or talking obscenely. Professor West's study found much the same. In 44 per cent of cases, there was physical contact stopping short of intercourse – touching, fondling, masturbation, oral sex – and in 5 per cent of cases there was intercourse, vaginal or anal.

In their study of the families referred to the sexual abuse treatment programme at Great Ormond Street Hospital between 1981 and 1986, Dr Arnon Bentovim and his colleagues found that the most common form of abuse was inappropriate fondling (65 per cent). Masturbation of an adult by a child (29 per cent) and partial sexual intercourse (28 per cent) were the next most common, followed by full vaginal intercourse (23 per cent) and anal intercourse (18 per cent). (In some cases, of course, a child has been abused in more than one way.) The children in this study had all been abused within the family, which obviously rules out abuse by strangers that involves no physical contact (for instance, indecent exposure and talking obscenely), and the abuse must have been considered serious for the family to have been referred to Great Ormond Street in the first place. Even so, it is an interesting fact that abuse involving penetration is still far less common than fondling. The NSPCC and Greater Manchester Authorities Child Sexual Abuse Unit in its first year of operation bears those findings out. They found that 36 per cent of the children they saw had been penetrated, while 59 per cent had been subjected to genital fondling or masturbation.

Richard Johnson, Director of Incest Crisis Line, which receives up to 1,500 calls a week from victims past and present, believes it is very important that people should understand the true picture. 'Being made to watch blue movies or being touched up as a kid is still unwanted sexual attention, a betrayal of trust often, and potentially damaging, although it's not as dramatic as rape. We're not scaremongers. We don't think you have to exaggerate the scale of the problem in order to draw attention to it – God knows, it's big enough as it is! We think that's counterproductive. If you make people think the problem is so big, nobody's going to want to work with it.'

WHO ARE THE VICTIMS?

The popular notion is that victims of sexual abuse are overwhelmingly girls, and while it is true that they make up the majority, various studies show that far more boys are sexually abused than people once thought. The MORI poll showed that of those people who had been victims of some form of sexual abuse as children, 40 per cent were male. Of the sexually abused children who contacted ChildLine in its first year, almost 25 per cent were boys. Dr Arnon Bentovim's Great Ormond Street study found the same. He also found that the abuse of boys was more severe – over half of them had been subjected to anal intercourse.

Another myth is that child sexual abuse most usually starts at or just after puberty – the 'Lolita syndrome'. Several American studies have found that for over half the people interviewed the abuse had already happened by the time they were twelve. The Great Ormond Street study found the percentage of children in each age group at which abuse started (3–5, 6–8, 9–11, 12–14) was more or less the same, around 22 per cent, with 3 per cent aged 15–16, and a mindboggling 5 per cent under the age of 3. The NSPCC's 1987 figures showed that the average age for sexually abused children is 9 years 8 months. The youngest sexually abused child Richard Johnson has ever come across was two weeks old.

You might expect abuse of very young children to be confined to the family – most parents simply do not let them out unaccompanied and so the opportunity for abuse by outsiders shouldn't arise. Sadly, that's not true. There are all too many cases of small children abused by babysitters, some of whom are only young teenagers or family 'friends', or by trusted professionals. There was a shocking case in California in 1983 where kindergarten teachers were accused of systematically abusing the under-fives in their charge. Seven of the teachers from the McMartin Pre-school in Manhattan Beach, California, were charged originally on 323 counts of child molestation. Eventually, in 1986, charges were dropped against five of the defendants, leaving two of them, a mother and son, to stand trial on 100 counts. The case, which has already cost Los Angeles County $8 million, is unlikely to be concluded before the end of 1988, but so seriously has the state of California taken the issues raised by the case that it has already pumped over $10 million into anti-sexual abuse programmes in its schools. Another consequence of the case is that male teachers have been banned from pre-school education throughout the USA – something of an over-reaction, surely, since not all men abuse children, and indeed some of those implicated in the McMartin case were women.

WHO ARE THE ABUSERS?

The popular view of child sexual abusers used to be of the furtive stranger in a dirty mac lurking outside school gates and using bribery with sweets to persuade children to go with him. Indeed early campaigns to try and protect children were founded on this premise – 'Never talk to strangers.' But then it became clear that many children were abused by people they knew, often by people within their own family, and the focus shifted from paedophiles who abuse children outside the home to the fathers, stepfathers, grandfathers, brothers and uncles within it. (Most abusers are male, though there are some females who abuse – between 1 and 10 per cent of the total.)

The prevailing view of whether this is mainly a family problem or a problem outside the family tends to depend on the most recent scandal. If it's a television documentary exposing child pornographers, then the focus shifts to paedophiles. If it's Cleveland, then it shifts back to the family again. According to the MORI poll, 49 per cent of victims (of which 44 per cent were girls and 57 per cent boys) knew their abuser. In view of the fact that over 50 per cent of the abuse reported was non-contact – 'flashing', obscene phone calls, and so on – and that this type of abuser almost always picks on strangers, that makes sense. Professor West's study of women who had been sexually abused in childhood found that 49 per cent did not know their abuser, a figure accounted for largely by the fact that many of the incidents involved 'flashers', which Professor West agrees is the most common female experience.

In cases of sexual abuse reported to the police, though, about 75 per cent of the children knew their abuser. It could well be that, although being flashed at can be a very frightening experience, many children or their parents don't think it's serious enough to report to the police.

MORI found that 14 per cent of all sexual abuse took place within the family, while in 35 per cent of cases the abuser was someone known to the child – teacher, neighbour, family 'friend', and so on. Diana Russell's 1983 study of 913 women in San Francisco found that of the 38 per cent who had been the victims of sexual abuse involving contact, only 11 per cent had been abused by total strangers; 29 per cent were abused by family members (and just under half of them, by their fathers); and the remaining 60 per cent were abused by people they knew. Of this last group of abusers, 40 per cent were 'authority figures'.

Perhaps a more useful distinction than that between abuse within the family or abuse outside it would be that between abuse by strangers and abuse by people known to and trusted by the child. It is the betrayal of trust that does the long-term damage, that causes the psychological scars that victims carry with them, often for the rest of their lives. For this reason Incest Crisis Line has broadened its working definition of incest from the traditional one of sexual intercourse with a close blood relation to include sexual abuse by stepfathers, adoptive fathers, mothers' boyfriends, friends' fathers, family friends, teachers, doctors . . . anyone, indeed, whom the child trusts.

Child sexual abuse is no respecter of class or race, although most statistics show that families in which children are abused tend to be working-class. In the Great Ormond Street study, 55 per cent of parents were in manual, partially skilled or unskilled jobs, and only 15 per cent were in higher clerical or professional jobs; 22 per cent had unemployment problems. But those findings are misleading. All the retrospective studies undertaken show no class bias at all – child sexual abuse goes right across the board. Incest Crisis Line finds that its clients have been abused by doctors, vicars, teachers, policemen, politicians, servicemen (officers and other ranks), senior civil servants, self-made men . . . Ray Wyre, a former probation officer and now a freelance lecturer and counsellor, has worked with many child sexual abusers over the last ten years and finds exactly the same social mix. His clients earlier this year included a barrister, a journalist and a headmaster.

The bias in statistics is most probably due to the fact that families on low incomes or on benefit are far more likely to come into contact with agencies like the social services and the police than middle-class families, and therefore abuse in those families is far more likely to be picked up. If there is any hint of suspicion that a middle-class father is abusing his own or other people's children, the notion that it is primarily a working-class problem, an opinion which even some professionals still hold, works in his favour. 'Oh, he wouldn't do a thing like that. He's such a nice, respectable man . . .'

Child psychiatrist Dr Eileen Vizard, a former member of the Great Ormond Street team, who is now setting up a child abuse treatment programme in the London Borough of Newham, is sometimes contacted by family doctors. 'They'll say, "I've got a really nice family where there's been just a bit of touching. Can you just give them a bit of family therapy? It's not the kind of case where we need to involve social services." I see that as an invitation to collude with the doctor and the family, to deny the problem, and I won't go along with it. I try to make the GP concerned accept what he is doing, which is trivializing the problem.'

If the suspicion is more than a hint, then a middle-class man is more likely than his working-class counterpart to have the know-how, the status and the money to keep himself out of the clutches of the statutory agencies – and the statistics.

Richard Johnson believes that where the alleged abuser is powerful, or even in the public eye, there is a deliberate policy not to prosecute. 'I believe that in 1987 the Director of Public Prosecutions decided to drop a case against a household name against whom there were well over a hundred allegations and photographic evidence. The attitude that seems to be coming from the DPP is that in cases like that "it is not in the public interest to prosecute", perhaps because it would undermine public confidence in the great and the good too much.'

As far as race is concerned, it seems that no group is immune. Studies carried out in the USA find no overall difference between whites and blacks in the level of child sexual abuse, though again there is some apparent bias in certain statistics because black families tend to suffer greater deprivation and therefore have more contact with official agencies than white families. Several studies suggested that Hispanic women (Spanish-speaking, and mainly of Puerto Rican origin) were victimized more often than either black or white women, while Diana Russell's study showed lower rates for Asian and Jewish women.

No similar studies have been carried out in this country. In the families referred to Great Ormond Street's sexual abuse treatment programme, 90 per cent of the adults were born in Britain and 90 per cent were white. Given that black people, Asians, Chinese, and people of mixed race make up about 6 per cent of this country's population, it might seem from those figures as though the incidence of child sexual abuse was higher in those groups. But again, the figures by themselves are misleading. Black families tend to suffer greater deprivation and are therefore more likely to be the focus of attention from statutory agencies for other reasons.

But while black families may have more enforced contact with the authorities, psychologist Maria Mars, who works with sexually abused children in a racially mixed London borough, believes that may well be balanced by the fact that they have less voluntary contact. 'There is always a conflict of loyalties for any child who's being abused, but it's even more difficult for black children. Most black people's experiences of social services and the police are negative, so a child has to decide whether to "betray" her family and her community by calling them, or whether to carry on putting up with the abuse.'

Dr Eileen Vizard works with sexually abused children in another racially mixed borough, Newham, and sees children from every religious and ethnic minority group. She makes the point that there are such marked differences between the groups that simply gauging the scale of the problem from those families who come into contact with the authorities is misleading. 'Some are much more tight-knit and self-contained than others. Third or fourth generation West Indian families, where the drive to integrate and yet maintain a

separate racial identity gets lots of the young people into trouble
with the authorities, are much more likely to be in contact with
agencies than, say, law-abiding Bengali families who generally keep
out of trouble and avoid contact with statutory services. So if child
sexual abuse was going on in those families, the various agencies are
less likely to hear about it.'

SOCIETY'S ATTITUDES

Despite the lack of clear evidence on the full extent of the
problem, there is no doubt that sexual abuse of children – of both
sexes, of all ages, from all sorts of backgrounds – flourishes in this
society. The key question is: Why? In later chapters, the motives of
abusers and the reasons for the victims' silence will be explored in
detail, but at this point it's worth looking at society's attitudes to
sexual abuse.

What is coming across is a very mixed message. On one level,
there is hysteria, outrage, disgust and loud demands that the authorities DO something. But on another level – the level of action rather
than words – the message is rather different. In one rate-capped
London borough, for instance, with a genuine commitment to
tackling child sexual abuse, they simply can't afford to pay enough
social workers to deal with all cases in which the evidence of sexual
abuse is incontrovertible, never mind those where there is only a
strong suspicion. In other areas, including Cleveland, it is proving
impossible to fill vacant posts, and the shortage of social workers is
chronic.

In one case where an eleven-year-old boy was sexually
abused by the parish priest, the police would not prosecute for 'lack
of evidence'. And the only action taken by the Church authorities
was to move the priest first to a retreat house and then to another
parish. The reaction in the community, where the priest was popular,
was to blame the family. The mother has lost friends because of it –
a couple of them won't even speak to her now – and the child has
been cruelly taunted at school. A jar of Vaseline was put in his
gym kit, and he has been provoked into any number of fights. In
another case, a child who disclosed that her father had been sex-

ually abusing her was smeared with excrement by adult neighbours.

Dianne Core, an ex-social worker and herself a victim of sexual abuse, founded and runs the Hull-based charity Childwatch, which offers not only telephone counselling to victims and their parents but also investigates cases in which the police have refused to prosecute – and is sometimes successful in making them change their minds. 'I had a case recently where a four-year-old girl had been seriously abused over an eight-month period by a family "friend". When the mother discovered what had happened she contacted the police, and though they were sympathetic, the powers that be wouldn't touch the case because of the child's age.' (The way the law currently stands, the uncorroborated evidence of a small child is not admissible in court and there are rarely any other witnesses.) 'She has subsequently been seen by a psychiatrist who is prepared to give evidence that the child has been sexually abused, but they still won't prosecute the man.'

In the last year or so we have become much more aware of, and outraged by, the prevalence of child pornography in this country, and quite rightly so. Leaving aside all libertarian arguments about the individual's right to read or see what he chooses to, child pornography is *always* the record of the sexual abuse of a child. Even when the acts are simulated, the experience is still an abusive one. At the beginning of 1988, the government announced that it was to make the mere possession of child pornography an offence punishable by a fine of up to £2,000. Before, only the production or distribution of it was an offence.

But in May 1987, paediatrician Dr Oliver Brook appealed successfully against the twelve-month jail sentence passed on him the previous December for dealing in child pornography. Brook had a collection containing over 3,000 items of child pornography, and in granting the appeal the most senior judge in the land, Lord Chief Justice Lane, said he was 'akin to a schoolboy collecting cigarette cards in olden times'. If that's the view of the judiciary, it's hard to imagine that they are going to crack down hard on other 'schoolboy' collectors.

What kind of message do children like these get about just how seriously society views child sexual abuse?

We express disgust at ten-year-old girls being made to look sexually provocative in pornographic pictures. But we don't object to them being made to look just as provocative in films, or fashion shots, or glossy advertisements for boots or costume jewellery. The tabloid press would be quick to label any forty-year-old man who had sex with a thirteen-year-old girl a 'monster'. But when the man was Rolling Stone Bill Wyman, and the girl Mandy Smith, the reaction was indulgent, amused, or even just a shade envious.

Ray Wyre, who works with sex offenders, quotes one particular edition of *Sunday Sport*: 'There were eight references to children as sex objects – from stories about Oliver Reed and his love for schoolgirls, Liberace and his love for boys, to a photograph of a thirteen-year-old "sex kitten". In the middle of all this was a piece by a psychologist saying that sex between girls and older men has a lot going for it.

'If there is anything in the tabloid press about sex with children, like the Bill Wyman story, practically every abuser I work with will show it to me the next day. They latch on to anything that "normalizes" or minimizes what they do. One of the hardest things in working with offenders is to break down the wall of denial, justification, minimization, "normalization", that they all erect around their activities. People just don't think about the effects of what they produce on sex offenders.'

Anne Bannister of the NSPCC in Manchester believes at the heart of the problem is the fact that society doesn't really condemn child sexual abuse. 'I think many people feel that, for girls anyway, and older girls especially, there's not a lot wrong with it. It's what's going to happen to them anyway, so whether they're over-age or under-age is largely immaterial, and besides, it doesn't really do any harm. I think these feelings are widespread throughout society for a variety of reasons. The main one is that people who abuse are actually very powerful indeed, and by that I mean they are in positions of power as well as powerful within their own little circle.

'The other reason has to do with our attitude to children in general. I believe all children are victimized to some extent. We all, we adults, abuse children because it is almost impossible to make boundaries when we are bringing them up. A child needs boundaries for its own safety, but the fine line to be drawn is between doing that and imposing your own personal power on that child for the sake of it.'

Michael Freeman, Professor of English Law at University College London and for years now a campaigner for children's rights, also believes that our general attitudes to children are at the root of the problem. 'What we tend to do is treat public problems as the private evils of children. Instead of tackling bad schools, we deal with truancy. Instead of tackling youth unemployment, we look at delinquency. In what other crime except child abuse do we decide that the main answer is to remove the victim, not the criminal, from the family home? You can't get rid of child abuse by locking up abusers. You have to ask, "What is wrong between all adults and children which permits this abuse to happen?"'

Few people would dispute that, as a society, we don't really like children very much. On a simplistic level, compare the experience of taking a baby or toddler into restaurants in this country and in Mediterranean countries. Here, a child is barely tolerated. There, it is the centre of attention, fussed over, played with, admired. On a more serious level, we were the last country in Europe to ban corporal punishment in state schools. We also lock up more children than any other European country. And it is quite impossible to imagine the situation ever arising here where parents were forbidden by law to beat their children, as they are in Sweden. We are extremely quick to defend parents' rights – witness Cleveland – but children's rights are given scant regard. According to Michael Freeman, in the area of children's rights 'no comparable country has a worse record than Britain'.

A BRITISH PROBLEM?

As far as child sexual abuse is concerned, though, we are certainly not alone. In countries like the USA, Canada and Australia, in northern Europe (Holland, Belgium, West Germany), and Scandinavia (Sweden, Denmark), the problem is acknowledged to be a major one. Many countries, for instance, now have helplines for victims.

Early in 1988 a study funded by the Irish Republic's Department of Health and Social Security found that one girl in four is sexually assaulted before she is eighteen and that the figure for boys is not much lower. The Department of Health rejected the report's findings out of hand, and although it stated that the report would be rewritten and published later, that didn't happen; so its author, Clodagh Corcoran, published the findings herself in a book called *Take Care!* (Poolbeg, Dublin, 1988).

In Holland, it is believed that one adult in ten has had an abusive experience in childhood. And last year there was visible and shocking evidence of the scale of child pornography in that country. Over seventy children between the ages of three and six were abducted from the small town of Oude Pekala by five men and two women dressed in clowns' costumes and masks. They were sexually abused and in some cases burnt with cigarettes, and the whole appalling business was recorded on film or video. The children were returned home after being threatened that if they told anyone, their mothers would be killed. The threats were so effective that it was only when one mother found burns on her daughter's body and consulted a doctor, and the police were called, that the incredible story began to emerge. The police believe the gang to be part of a much bigger, highly lucrative child pornography operation, but one year later no charges have been brought and the police consider the case closed.

In West Germany, the Union for the Protection of Children (the equivalent of the NSPCC) reported 12,000 cases of child sexual abuse – over double the number on child abuse registers in England and Wales. There is no reason to suppose that those figures aren't just the tip of the iceberg, as ours are.

France has never done a national survey on child sexual abuse and has no plans to, but an estimated 50–60,000 children a year are abused either physically or sexually.

While most Italians are still proud of their country's reputation for loving children and deny that abuse is a problem, the facts don't bear that out. A children's judge in Naples was quoted recently as saying that 10 per cent of the cases she deals with involve child prostitutes operating with the consent of their families. An Italian psychiatrist, Ernesto Coffo, has just established a 24-hour telephone helpline, SOS Infancy, for parents and children in danger, which presumably he wouldn't have done if there had been no need for it.

As an indication of the geographical spread of the problem, at a conference in Rhodes last year organized by the International Association for the Study and Prevention of Child Abuse and Neglect, papers on various aspects of incest and child sexual abuse in general were given by delegates from France, Germany, Italy, Greece, Bulgaria, Israel, Finland and Scandinavia, as well as from this country, the Irish Republic and the USA.

In third world countries, there is a variety of different cultural patterns. In some Muslim countries where unmarried girls are closely guarded, the sexual abuse of young boys, particularly as prostitutes, is common. The same is true in Sri Lanka, where in the 1970s, according to Judith Ennew, author of *The Sexual Exploitation of Children* (Polity Press, Cambridge, 1986), there were 2,000 boy prostitutes between the ages of seven and seventeen catering to the 'sex tourism' market. In Thailand, as a recent television documentary showed, and the Philippines, 'sex tourism' also flourishes, with thousands of young prostitutes of both sexes. But whether it is simply a matter of demand creating the supply or whether the sexual abuse of children is integral to the cultures of those countries, no one knows.

Not surprisingly, very little work has been done by anthropologists on sexual abuse in other cultures. After all, it is only really in the last ten years or so that its prevalence has been acknowledged in the West, and in countries where simply finding enough food each day to keep a child alive is the primary concern, sexual abuse has a very low priority.

A collection of anthropological essays edited by Jill E. Korbin, *Child Abuse and Neglect: Cross Cultural Perspectives* (University of California Press, 1981), touches on it, though it concentrates on physical abuse in places like New Guinea, sub-Saharan Africa, Japan and China. She makes the point that it is important to look at what is considered abusive in each culture. We are horrified by initiation rites involving circumcision, male and female, in North Africa, or oral and anal sex among the young males of some tribes in New Guinea, but people in those communities consider these practices essential if their children are to grow up and take their place as adults in the community. Indeed, they would consider it abusive *not* to allow their children to go through initiation rites. And they would consider our practice of putting babies to sleep in separate rooms, or smacking toddlers, abusive in the extreme.

Jill Korbin also makes the general point that societies where the extended family is the norm – lots of aunts, uncles, grandparents and cousins all living within a stone's throw of each other and all sharing the care of and responsibility for the children – offer a child more protection from abuse than Western societies where most children grow up just with their biological parents or parent, and have no wider network of adults concerned about their welfare. Such societies offer not only protection against abuse within the family but also protection against abuse by strangers, in that there is always an adult or older child around keeping an eye on the children; since the communities tend to be fairly small, it is relatively easy for potential abusers to be identified and the word passed around.

The contributors to Jill Korbin's book found little evidence of child abuse as we know it, either physical or sexual, in many of the cultures they looked at. But in some parts of sub-Saharan Africa there was evidence of sexual abuse of young girls by fathers and by their close relatives, though incest is usually considered a religious rather than a civil offence (indeed the same was true in this country until 1908, when incest became a criminal offence). In Nigeria and Kenya there are recurrent scandals about teachers seducing pubescent pupils and losing their jobs as a result. The authors of this particular essay, Sarah and Robert Le Vine, state that 'it is our impression moreover that both battering and sexual molestation are more common where the impact of social change is conspicuous'.

In rural Turkey, there is much open admiration and touching of small children's genitals. In Taiwan, there were scandals about the abuse, sexual and physical, of 'foster daughters-in-law' – orphans or girls from very poor families adopted basically as cheap labour in the home – which led to legislation specifically to protect them in the mid seventies.

There seems little evidence of child sexual abuse in China and Japan, though it's worth noting that the overwhelming majority of Japanese tourists visiting the Philippines, renowned for its 'sex tourism', are male. In *The Sexual Exploitation of Children*, Judith Ennew writes:

At least two studies have suggested that men are more likely to sample sexual activities with children, or give way to repressed paedophilic tendencies, while away from home. Not only does the fact of being on holiday give the individual greater licence, but also the rules of another society do not have so great a deterrent effect as those in which one was socialized.

In looking at other countries and cultures, it is worth remembering that because no one has yet uncovered evidence of widespread child sexual abuse, this doesn't mean that it doesn't exist. As American psychiatrist and specialist in child sexual abuse Suzanne Sgroi has put it, 'Absence of proof is not proof of absence.'

No culture on earth approves of incest or the abuse of a small child by an adult for his or her own sexual gratification, and so where it does happen, it happens in secret. If you had asked for information about the scale of the problem in this country even ten years ago, you would have been told that it was pretty small.

WHY NOW?

Given that we know child sexual abuse is not a new phenomenon – the retrospective studies make that patently clear – why has it exploded into public consciousness in the last few years?

There are a number of reasons. First, though it seems as though it has always been with us, it is only twenty years since Henry Kempe first identified the 'battered baby syndrome', and it took quite some time before the extent of the physical abuse of children became widely accepted. People in general, and some professionals, at first found it almost impossible to accept that parents, and especially mothers, could inflict such terrible injuries on their own children. But it did become an accepted fact, along with an attitude that in many cases battering could be prevented if the stress the parents were under was acknowledged and help given in time. The NSPCC and voluntary organizations like Parents Anonymous offered a safety valve and enabled many parents in danger of injuring their children to come forward seeking help, knowing they would not be punished or blamed.

As professionals became more skilled in identifying the physical and emotional signs of physical abuse, they began to pick up evidence of sexual abuse too. Dr Arnon Bentovim and his colleagues at Great Ormond Street found that at least 15 per cent of sexually abused children had also been physically abused. And while it is often said that sexual abuse, unlike physical abuse, is not life-threatening, there have been suggestions that some children killed by their parents have been sexually as well as physically abused. Judy Keshet-Orr, who now runs an incest intervention programme in north London, started her working life as a social worker in the 1970s. 'I often found when I started working with "difficult" families, presenting with problems of physical abuse, that there was sexual abuse too. Mothers who abused their kids physically or were unable to prevent them from being abused sexually, had often been sexually abused as children. What I was seeing was literally a knock-on effect.'

The growth of the women's movement, and particularly the setting-up of rape crisis centres all over the country, also played an important part in exposing the extent of child sexual abuse to the public gaze. Women who contacted a rape crisis centre after a sexual assault often revealed that they had also been sexually abused as children. Once the work of such centres became more widely known, other women rang simply to talk about their childhood experiences.

Incest Crisis Line was founded in 1980 by a single mother with four children, who had been sexually abused as a child and who now prefers not to be named. An enlightened GP, new to the practice where she was registered, chose not to continue prescribing Valium for her depression, but listened to her childhood experiences and then introduced her to six other women patients in the same situation. They all found the informal group that resulted so valuable that they decided to try to do something to help other people in the same boat, and started a helpline from one of their houses. To begin with they got very few calls, so they decided to publicize their existence and persuaded the local paper to carry a small story. The result of that was 3,000 calls in ten days. The phone rang non-stop, twenty-four hours a day, until – literally! – the bell fell off.

Slowly they began to expand the helplines and also started to campaign for a better deal for victims. In 1982, Richard Johnson, then working as a milkman, contacted them to seek help for his niece, who had been sexually abused by her father, his half-brother (see p. 118). They helped her, and persuaded him to train as a counsellor. After a couple of years it became known that there was this '6' 3" tall, cockney ex-prostitute, ex-boxer, ex-milkman, ex-tube-driver', as he describes himself, who was prepared to get up in public and say that he had been raped by his father for most of his childhood. The media had become rather bored with female victims talking about rape, but a male victim – and a victim of incest, too – was news. He was invited to appear on television programmes, to the benefit of both parties: the television companies got sensational material, and the plight of incest victims, as well as the existence of Incest Crisis Line, got invaluable publicity.

It also showed people who had been, and were being, sexually abused that it is possible to survive the experience and not remain victims all their lives. And a high media profile has undoubtedly given Richard Johnson access to people in positions of power, who can get things done.

FACT OR FANTASY?

From the experience of rape crisis centres and Incest Crisis Line, it is clear that although many people had never told anyone what had happened to them, those who *had* tried to tell were usually not believed – not simply by parents or other trusted adults, but by professionals.

The reason, largely, was Sigmund Freud's theories of infantile sexuality and the Oedipus complex which he developed in the late 1890s, and which explained childhood sexual experiences in terms of their existence only in the child's fantasy. The child *wanted* a sexual relationship with his or her parent, and so in his or her mind it had actually happened. But in 1896, a year or two before he published those theories, he had given a lecture called 'The Aetiology of Hysteria'. In it he described his findings that, in eighteen cases of previously unexplained hysterical illness referred to him, each patient had been sexually abused in childhood either by an adult or by an older brother or sister. None of the patients had been aware of this when they first went to see Freud; it only emerged during the course of analysis. The lecture caused such an outcry that in the following year, 1897, Freud disowned it. In its place he came up with his theories of infantile sexuality and the Oedipus complex.

They influenced most medical practitioners for the next sixty years or more. Children who claimed to have been sexually abused by someone they knew were making it up. If there was incontrovertible physical proof that they weren't – a sexually transmitted disease or a pregnancy, for example – the view generally was that the fantasies were so powerful that they had spilled over into reality and the children had initiated the sexual contact themselves.

That attitude has by no means disappeared. In an incest case in the USA not so long ago the defence convinced sufficient members of the jury that the child was so promiscuous she had led her father on, so that it was unable to reach a verdict. The child was three and a half years old.

Even when more and more evidence was produced to show that Freud had been right the first time, the notion still lingered that children who alleged they had been sexually abused were lying. In fact there is a growing body of evidence to show that children very rarely lie about sexual abuse. One American study showed that of 690 allegations of sexual abuse, only twenty-one turned out to be false. Fifteen of them involved teenagers and four involved younger children where divorcing parents were engaged in bitter custody battles and the children had been 'coached' in their stories. That leaves only two cases out of 690 where children (both under the age of twelve) had just made it up.

Psychologist Gerrilyn Smith has had a lot of experience in child sexual abuse cases. 'I have never come across a child who told an out-and-out lie about having been abused. I've had confused presentations, I've had children name someone else in order to protect the person who had really abused them, and I've known children describe it as though it was happening at one time when it actually happened at another. But an out-and-out lie, never.

'Children don't make "false allegations". They tell you about their experiences and it's the legal system which makes them into allegations. There was an example of a child making a "false allegation". A little girl in a foster family told her teacher she was "frenched" by her foster father. The foster father had had a stroke and his tongue protruded, so when he kissed the child his tongue was out. That child was simply describing her experiences, and because of her history it was taken up in a particular way. When there was found to be no abuse, it was labelled a "false allegation" and the child treated as a liar.'

Richard Johnson's experience is much the same. 'Kids very, very rarely lie about being abused and it's very easy to tell if they do. They might be able to say "He stuck it in me" if it hadn't happened, but they wouldn't be able to describe what it felt like, or their emotions.'

A combination of information from the various self-help groups, as well as research carried out in other countries and work being done by teams like that at Great Ormond Street, led to some members of the caring professions – doctors, social workers, and so on – becoming much more aware of the prevalence of child sexual abuse. They began to consider it as a possible explanation for a whole range of conditions that previously they hadn't been able to account for – persistent urinary or vaginal infections in very young girls, for example, 'tummy-aches' with no apparent cause, sleeping and eating difficulties, and a whole range of problems with behaviour.

Once they started looking for it, they began to find cases of child sexual abuse in large numbers. In Leeds, for instance, the cases of suspected sexual abuse referred to the city's paediatricians went from none in 1979, to 7 in 1982, to 161 (and confirmed or thought probable in 106 cases) in 1985, to over 900 in 1986 with 274 of the latter confirmed.

In October 1986, two Leeds paediatricians, Dr Jane Wynne and Dr Christopher Hobbs, published a paper in the *Lancet* called 'Buggery in Childhood – a common syndrome of child abuse', in which they described buggery (anal intercourse) in young children as a 'serious, common and under-reported type of child abuse'. In an eight-month period between October 1985 and May 1986, they saw 35 children (18 girls and 17 boys) between the ages of fourteen months and eight years, 24 of them under the age of five, in whom they diagnosed sexual abuse, including buggery. In their paper they also described the diagnostic technique that was to become notorious in the Cleveland affair – reflex anal dilatation or R A D – in which the child's buttocks are gently parted, and any subsequent involuntary relaxation of the sphincter (the ring of muscles at the entrance to the anus) noted. They also described the sort of abnormalities that are also usually present – anal fissures or cracks, for example, and swelling of the veins – but went on to make the point that they had 'not seen severe lacerations, bruises or anal disruption in any case, and we therefore think these are not the usual signs of anal abuse even in very young children'. If the abnormalities they described had been congenital, Drs Hobbs and Wynne presumed they would have been noted at birth. They also stated that, in their opinion, such abnormalities are seldom caused by disease or constipation. While they say that the physical signs (dilatation – the anus permanently opened – RAD, and swelling of the veins), if they are gross enough, can be sufficient to make a diagnosis, usually the physical evidence should be only one factor, along with 'associated evidence – particularly explicit behaviour manifest in the child's play. *Of greatest importance is a clear history given by the child of interference with his bottom.*' (My italics.) As we have seen, it was their methods which Dr Higgs adopted in the North-East, so sparking off the whole Cleveland controversy.

In the aftermath of Cleveland, some parents of children in Leeds who had been diagnosed as having been sexually abused demanded second opinions, and in the spring of 1988 both Drs Hobbs and Wynne threatened to resign, blaming pressure and a media witch-hunt. As Dr Hobbs put it, 'Unless there is support for this work and there is a considered view that it must go on, I must find another field to work in.'

While accepting that all doctors can, and do, make mistakes, and again not minimizing the terrible damage done to children and families when sexual abuse is wrongly diagnosed, the ferocity of the outcry against these doctors, the scapegoating, goes much further than that. It has faint echoes of the outcry against Freud's theories in Vienna in 1896. As a result of that, as we know, the whole issue of child sexual abuse was largely swept under the carpet for the next sixty or seventy years, with devastating results for its many victims. It would be tragic – and unforgivable – if history were allowed to repeat itself in the 1980s.

2 Victims

THE DAMAGE DONE

Whoever they are, whatever gender they are, there seems little doubt that the effects of sexual abuse on its victims, both short-term and long-term, can be very damaging indeed. The statistics present a horrifying picture. In this country, an estimated 75–80 per cent of female street prostitutes, for example, and almost all male prostitutes, were sexually abused as children. So were between 60 per cent and 80 per cent of adolescents, male and female, who attempt suicide, 75 per cent of chronic runaways, 44 per cent of drug addicts, 40 per cent of all prison inmates (in the USA the figure is thought to be up to 70 per cent or more), 40 per cent of all children in care, and, according to conversations Richard Johnson of Incest Crisis Line has had with doctors and psychiatrists, 75 per cent of anorexics, and a large percentage of young people diagnosed as schizophrenic . . . the list goes on and on. Behind those statistics lies a pool of human misery, of potential blighted, of opportunities lost and lives destroyed, of failed relationships and fraught, unhappy parenthood.

While it is true to say that a sexually abusive experience is always damaging to a child, the degree of damage varies enormously according to a whole range of factors. But the experts in the field are by no means unanimous about what these are. Some believe the length of time the abuse continues is extremely important. A one-off incident – being flashed at, having a stranger make obscene suggestions to you – is obviously much less likely to cause serious problems than abuse that goes on for a number of years. Others believe the type of abuse makes a difference, too, and that penetration, either anal, vaginal or oral, is more damaging than masturbation or fondling. 'I have a clinical sense,' said child psychiatrist Dr Eileen Vizard, 'that when children's bodies are penetrated in that way it is more harmful than other forms of abuse because their mind is also being penetrated, fragmented and attacked in a very concrete way.

But that is not to say that other types of abuse are not potentially very damaging.'

Other experts believe the age of the child is important. Some argue that more damage is done to very young children who cannot make sense of the experience, while others believe that children who are old enough to understand the taboos that have been broken are harmed the most. A large age gap between the victim and abuser – at least five years if the victim is under fourteen, ten years if she is older – is seen as damaging by some experts, though recent research in the USA points to quite serious damage resulting from abuse in childhood by peers who are only a year or two older. There has been some research which suggests that when the abuse is accompanied by violence, the damage done is greater, and there is yet another school of thought which maintains that if the abuser used violence to overcome any resistance, the child feels less responsible for what happened than she might if the forms of pressure employed were more subtle. On one thing, though, all the experts are unanimous. The closer the relationship between victim and abuser, the more damaging the abuse is likely to be, whether it involves penetration or not, for what lies at the heart of it is the betrayal of a most fundamental trust. A child, by definition, relies on the adults in her life – parents, close relatives, family friends, teachers, doctors, priests – for security and protection from harm, but if they themselves are harming the child, she feels confused, powerless and totally vulnerable.

Because betrayal of trust leaves no visible marks, many people still find it hard to accept how damaging it can be, as Dr Eileen Vizard finds sometimes when she is called as an expert witness in court cases. 'Barristers get up on their hind legs and start saying, "Oh, come on, doctor, there's just been a bit of fondling here. You're not trying to tell me that could hurt a child?" You then have to try and explain that, in this context, more important than the damage done to the child's body is the damage done to his or her mind. It is the most tremendous betrayal of the child's trust if their genital regions are invaded in that way.'

Another very damaging factor, when sexual abuse occurs within the family, is the secrecy that surrounds it. Children who are sexually assaulted by a stranger can usually tell their parents, though sometimes they may be reluctant to do so – if they've been playing where they have been forbidden to play, for example, or if they have often been warned about talking to strangers.

Of the sexually abused children who ring ChildLine, only 3 per cent have been abused by strangers. The remaining 97 per cent, who have been sexually abused by a member of their family, very often feel that they can tell no one they know. The abuser tells them it's 'their secret' which they mustn't tell anyone, and children feel a very strong obligation to keep secrets. Sometimes they are threatened with violence, told that they or their parents will be killed if they tell, as in the extraordinary affair at Oude Pekala in Holland (see p. 22).

More commonly, though, children are threatened with the consequences of telling. They'll get into trouble, they might be taken away, the family would have to move house and dad would lose his job, no one would love them any more, no one would believe them and nobody likes liars, the abuser might be put in prison. Children who call ChildLine are clearly frightened of the possible consequences of disclosing what's been going on, which explains why over 95 per cent of them give only their first name so that there is no chance they can be identified and the authorities informed.

Hard though it is for people with no experience of abuse to believe it, most abused children hate the abuse but still love the person who abuses them – the 'good daddy/monster daddy' syndrome – and don't want him to be sent to prison. 'You also have to remember,' said Valerie Howarth, director of ChildLine, 'that a child's primary family is usually all they've got, their total security. If you put yourself back into your own childhood and think what it would have been like, even on the very worst days, to lose your family, then perhaps you can understand their feelings a little more.'

Other children feel an overwhelming need to protect their mothers. Maria's father, used to beat her mother and her four brothers and sisters, as well as sexually abusing her. Maria felt her mother 'had more than enough to do, coping with her own problems, without me adding to them. Anyway, if I had told her what he was doing, there was nothing she could have done – she had been so beaten down physically and emotionally that she had no inner strength left. It was only after my fourth suicide attempt, when I wound up in a psychiatric hospital, that the doctors insisted I told her what had gone on. I didn't want to – she'd suffered enough – but they made me. It was pretty bad because of course she blamed herself.'

Since the abuser often stresses that the child will get into trouble if it all comes out, she assumes that she must have done wrong. Then her own sense of guilt as well as fear of the consequences ensure that she will keep the secret.

Guilt is a very powerful emotion and extremely common among victims of abuse, even when it is (and it invariably is) wholly irrational. Even though sexual abuse is never, ever a child's fault, many still blame themselves, even as adults, for 'allowing' it to happen.

Many abused children develop strategies for their own survival, but they don't recognize these for what they are and blame themselves for what has happened. Take Tracy. She's fifteen and trying to study for her GCSEs, 'O'-levels, though her ability to concentrate is severely limited by the fact that she has been regularly sexually abused by her father for some time. The sixth sense that sexually abused children develop tells her when she walks into the house whether tonight will be one of those nights when he is in the mood. Rather than sit waiting, unable to concentrate on any school work, for the creak on the stairs and for her father to appear in her room, she goes downstairs, takes her clothes off and sits on his lap. At least it's under her control. After it's over, she can go back to her room and get on with her homework in peace.

ESTIMATING THE DAMAGE

Although Anne Bannister of the NSPCC in Manchester accepts that the closeness of the relationship between the victim and the abuser is an important factor in the long-term consequences of sexual abuse, she maintains that you can't gauge who will recover from the experience and who won't from the nature of the abuse itself or from who did it: 'You have to know a whole lot more about the person concerned before you can say. One woman I know had a very harsh upbringing. Her father never abused her physically or sexually, but he gave nothing emotionally apart from criticism. Her mother was also terrified of the father and gave the child nothing either.

'When she was ten she became friendly with a young woman married to a much older man. They had a baby, with whom the ten-year-old used to help. Sometimes she was alone with the husband, and he abused her for two or three years. He didn't penetrate her, he fondled her. So there you have a child who'd been fondled but never penetrated or been asked for masturbation or oral sex, and an abuser who was not a family member, so you might feel she had been abused only mildly. But the damage done to that woman is enormous. She keeps saying, "But why did I keep going back to the house? It must be my fault, and my dad was right – I am wicked." What she can't accept is that she had no option. She needed affection, as all children need affection if they are going to survive, and if they don't get it at home, they will seek it anywhere. I'm not saying that she wouldn't have been damaged without the abuse, but if she'd met a young man, fallen in love, done all the normal things, she might well have been fine. As it was, the sexual abuse compounded the damage already done to her as a child.'

On paper, Kathy's experiences may sound pretty mild too. From the age of five she had been first 'tickled', then fondled, by an uncle. 'When his hands started to wander, he said, "It's all right, you don't have to worry. I do this with a girl down the road all the time. I feels her like this" – he tried to fondle my breasts – "and she feels me like this" – he tried to push my hand to his groin – "I gives her money and she's quite happy." I learnt later that he already had a conviction for child molesting, and yet my parents still let him visit our house. That stopped when I was about twelve – I just used to avoid him when he came to the house.

'Then when I was fourteen, I was sitting on the sofa one day with my father. Suddenly he was on top of me, fully clothed, but pushing away for all he was worth. I told him to get off, and he did because he heard mum coming. That's all it was, and yet the effect on me has been devastating. My uncle always said that if I ever told anyone what "we" had been doing, I'd get into trouble, so it had to be my fault. And the fact that it happened twice confirmed that it must be something about me.

'Although it was only the once with him, what my dad did

was more damaging than what my uncle had done. Dad had been the one I'd looked up to, the one I'd go to with any problems, the one I always felt I could trust with my life, and all that disappeared in an instant.'

If the abuse starts when a child is very young, she may not perceive it as abuse at all. Sue had lived alone with her mother until, when she was eight, her stepfather appeared on the scene. 'Not having had a dad before, I didn't know what dads were supposed to do, so I just accepted what he was doing without question. By the time I did begin to realize it was wrong, it had been going on for so long that I felt I was in it up to my neck. I just didn't see how I could tell anyone without getting into terrible trouble.'

Jane, who is now eighteen, and her three sisters were dominated by their father to such an extent that they were never allowed to make friends or to go to anyone else's home, so until she was thirteen and started sex education lessons at school, she assumed that the sexual and physical abuse she suffered at his hands was simply part of normal family life.

Sally doesn't remember exactly when her father, a regular army officer, started abusing her, but she's sure it was before she was four. 'He used to say that what he did to me was a very special kind of love between us. I remember once, when I was four, he beat me with a slipper and made it into some sort of ceremony with my brother and sister watching. It really bothered me then – I was totally confused – and it has done ever since. I think now I understand why I was so confused. On the one hand we were supposed to have this "very special kind of love" between us and yet on the other he was beating me in a rather sadistic way.

I don't know when I first realized it was wrong. Certainly I remember spending Christmas with relatives when I was twelve, and he tried it there, but when someone came into the room he jumped back very guiltily. I'm sure I had a very good idea, before that, that it was wrong, but afterwards I knew for sure.'

Paula, who is now in her late thirties, asked her mother what periods were when she was nine years old. Soon after, her father started touching her vagina and explaining what it was for, and then masturbated in front of her to show her what semen was like. 'He told me that he was giving me sex education and I thought that's how it was.'

Even now, at the age of twenty-eight, Simon doesn't accept that what happened to him was sexual abuse. 'I suppose you could say I was taken advantage of by someone old enough to know better. When I was twelve I was seduced by our live-in housekeeper who was thirty and had a small child of her own. It started harmlessly enough – her tucking me up in bed, running her fingers through my hair, and so on – and then it gradually progressed to her fondling my genitals, then to oral sex and full intercourse. I knew it was "naughty" in the way that nude pictures and *Playboy* were naughty, but it was tremendously exciting, and for a long time I didn't feel any guilt. And when I did, I still don't know whether it was moral guilt or performance-related guilt. I can remember her saying, "Oh, why did you come then? We could have gone on for hours!" What had been a pleasant, sensual experience turned into a situation where there was a great deal of lust, desire to penetrate her, and yet great anxiety about not being able to satisfy her.'

THE ONSET OF GUILT

Other children know from the start that what's happening is wrong, even if they don't understand why.

'I knew from the way my father used to creep into the room I shared with my sister at night and "shush" me that it was wrong,' said Sarah, who is now in her early forties. 'He used to get up at 5 a.m. for work, so he'd go to bed very early, leaving my mother downstairs. He'd take me into their bed, fondle my genitals and make me hold his, and then when he was finished he'd say, "Go back to bed and don't tell mummy." Once, I remember getting very frightened and threatening to tell her. He was absolutely terrified, and even said he'd kill himself. And I suppose I thought that what was going on was obviously so dreadfully wrong that I couldn't tell anyone.'

For other children, the realization that what had been happening was wrong came later, even though it may well have been painful, unpleasant or had made them feel very uncomfortable for some time.

Anne, whose stepfather married her mother when she was about two, doesn't know exactly when he started abusing her, but she can't remember a time when it wasn't happening. 'Mum was working and he wasn't, so he'd get me up in the mornings, wash me – and take an awful long time about it. I didn't know there was anything wrong with that. Everyone in our house walked around naked – mum thought it would be good for me to learn not to be ashamed of my body. One day I remember, after we'd had a bath together, he had an erection, and he called me over to where he was standing and told me to give him a kiss. When I got there his penis came up and hit me under the chin. All three of us, him, mum and I, thought it was hysterical and we fell about laughing!

'At first, it was just fondling – "our game" he called it, and he wasn't nasty to me. But then he started to get more adventurous, wanting first to have oral sex and make me swallow his semen, and then full intercourse. I started to feel frightened and uncomfortable, and tried to say no, and then he did get really vicious. He'd beat me often. Once, when he wanted sex and I was crying and saying I didn't want to, he took my pet hamster out of her cage and held her out of the window, saying he'd drop her if I didn't do what he wanted. I gave in, but the hamster died anyway – from fright, I imagine. I was about eight.'

Anne is convinced that her mother didn't know, although she says her behaviour must have given some indication that something was wrong. She was frightened to get up in the night to go to the lavatory in case her stepfather heard her, so she sometimes soiled or wet the bed. She would try all sorts of tactics to stop her mother from going to work and leaving her alone with him. Once she deliberately put her hand on a red-hot ring on the electric cooker. At school she vacillated between being submissive in the extreme so that she was bullied by the other children and having severe tantrums – one day in a lesson about dinosaurs, she scribbled all over her text-books, flung a chair across the room and ran out and locked herself in the lavatory. 'Mum had been working late the previous night, and I'd had his undivided attention for the whole evening. That's what that little outburst was all about, but nobody even suspected anything was wrong at home.'

Both types of behaviour – extreme submissiveness and temper tantrums – are common in sexually abused children. For other children school is a refuge, the only place where they are safe. It's not

uncommon for them to cry in the afternoons because they know it
will soon be time to go home.

Many abused children are loners, and have few friends at
school. For some there is the fear that other children will find out
what's going on and taunt them. But many simply feel that they are
not like other children; indeed, that they are no longer children
themselves. 'You hear other girls talking about sex and giggling,'
said Anne, 'even later on boasting that they've done it when you
know perfectly well from what they're saying that they haven't. But
you envy them their innocence. I remember one girl telling me
about her boyfriend and how they were slowly working their way
towards doing it. The day she told me they'd done it, I thought,
"You lucky cow!" OK, it had been the usual first-time disaster, but
at least they'd done it the right way.'

Mike, who is now twenty-eight and who was abused by an
uncle from the age of eight until he was fourteen, was a loner at
school. 'If anyone tried to be friendly, I couldn't be sure whether
they really liked me or whether there was an ulterior motive. I didn't
trust anyone, so basically I didn't mix. I stayed well clear.'

Some children are simply forbidden to make friends at school,
and as they get older, of course, boyfriends are out of the question.

Sarah's father was fiercely possessive of her in her teens. He
found out that she used to meet a boy she became very fond of in a
coffee bar after school, and he'd spy on her. 'If he found us together,
he'd beat me. When I was fifteen, the whole family emigrated to
South Africa. I shared a cabin with my mother, while my father
shared with my brothers. But he'd be lying in my bunk every night
at ten o'clock to make sure I came in at the time he'd stipulated. At
one point I did ask my mother why she let him behave like this and
she said, "He's only doing it to protect you from the men on the
ship." I was sorely tempted to say, "I'm in far greater need of
protection from him than from any other man", but I didn't.' Sarah
had also found it impossible to explain what must have seemed like
rather odd behaviour to her boyfriend. 'I daren't tell him. I was
afraid he would blame me.'

The capacity to trust anyone – child or adult – is, understandably, destroyed in many sexually abused children. When Sue (see p.
36) was eleven, her behaviour was so disturbed that it was decided to

introduce her to her real father, who had left home when she was only a few months old, for the first time, to see if that would solve her problems. 'We were getting on really well until we went to his house and he said, "Come on then! Come and sit on your dad's lap and give him a cuddle!" I thought, "Oh no. Not again", and I just froze. If I hadn't frozen, if I hadn't been afraid to be alone with him, I could well have developed a good relationship with him. When it all came out in the open a couple of years later and I was packed off by my mum, I might even have found a home with him and his new family. But of course, none of that happened.'

Not surprisingly, since that is what their experience has programmed them to do, sexually abused children often behave in a sexually explicit way. They masturbate openly and frequently, try to fondle other children – one two-and-a-half-year-old girl in a nursery school, as well as masturbating herself, pulled down a boy's pants and pushed her finger up his bottom. They talk about sex in a way that isn't appropriate for their age – one six-year-old boy asked a teacher if he would like him to 'suck his willie and make the milk come out'; they draw explicit pictures, or attempt to play aggressively sexual games in the playground.

Sue's mother was asked to go up to the school when she was about thirteen. 'The teacher said I was obviously very sexually aware – with an adult's attitude to sex, not a child's – and they didn't know why. The school suggested a psychiatrist, but before the appointment could be kept, it all came out in the open.'

SEXUAL BEHAVIOUR

The very real danger for children who have become sexualized much too early is that they unwittingly attract other abusers and so become victims all over again.

Anne's mother left her stepfather when Anne was eight (see p. 37) and moved into a house divided into bedsitters. 'I was very wary of men and couldn't stand them near me, something I made pretty plain. But there was a guy living there called Tony who was really kind to me. At first he just talked to me, and let me play his tapes in the communal living-room. Then I started going to his room and eventually things started to happen. He used to take my clothes off and look at me. Then he'd take his clothes off and ask me to look at him. Sometimes he'd cuddle me and tell me he loved me, but he never hurt me, never forced me, or even asked me, to do anything to him. It all came out because he used to take polaroid pictures of me naked and, using the timer, of the two of us naked together. Eventually, one of the other tenants found them.

'I suppose I knew it was wrong, but I was fond of Tony; he gave me the affection that no one else did and I didn't want to get him into trouble. Later on, the fact that it had happened to me twice meant it was most definitely my fault. Once could have been just bad luck, but twice . . .'

Some children develop a hatred of themselves that results in self-destructive impulses. They attempt suicide – in many cases, several times – or they injure themselves, cutting their arms, faces, legs, with razor blades or broken glass.

Other children's behaviour is less dramatic but self-destructive none the less. They abuse drugs and alcohol, or run away from home with all the risks that that involves. One study in Arizona found that 55 per cent of runaways and truants had been sexually abused.

From the age of thirteen Anne ran away any number of times. 'I used to go to Leicester Square, pick up a bloke outside the disco, get him to take me in, buy me drinks and then I would sleep with him, just to have a bed for the night. It didn't bother me – sex meant nothing. People asked me why I kept running away, but I couldn't tell them. I just couldn't bear being in the same house as my mum's new bloke – not that he ever laid a finger on me and I know he never would. But any man in that position was too close for comfort, as far as I was concerned.'

Other sexually abused children suffer from mystery illnesses – at least, illnesses that are a mystery to everyone else.

Sue used to be sick every Sunday night. 'Weekends were OK because mum was there all the time, but on Mondays she'd go back to work and I knew that when I got home from school he'd be there. Eventually the doctor sent me to hospital, and they poked and prodded in every place except the right one. They said they could find nothing wrong. It was probably nerves. In a twelve-year-old?'

Sarah was absolutely terrified of male teachers at school, and if she ever found herself alone with one she would break into a cold sweat and start shaking. 'I felt there was something about me, something in my eyes, that made men touch me, so I'd never look at them. If anyone showed me any kindness, I was terrified. One day a very nice, perfectly harmless male teacher offered to walk part of the way home with me, but I was so frightened that I made some pathetic excuse and hurried away. He obviously noticed my behaviour was odd, because a few days later he asked me if he frightened me. But of course I couldn't tell him what was wrong.'

Eating difficulties are also common. Either children overeat and become obese – presumably in order to provide a protective covering and make themselves as unattractive as possible – or they go to the other extreme and become anorexic. One study on eating disorders (anorexia and bulimia nervosa) carried out in this country in 1984 found that 34 per cent of the sample had been sexually abused before the age of fifteen. Other people believe the number is much higher.

Many victims suffer from sleep disorders – fear of going to bed, nightmares, bedwetting, and so on. Paula woke a few times and found her father already in her bed. 'It was terrifying, and not surprisingly I found it extremely difficult to sleep after that. I still find it hard. The slightest noise will wake me.'

Anne Bannister believes that many of the outward signs that abused children display are very obvious pointers to what is wrong, if only adults would see them. 'Is it surprising that a child who is abused in its bed at night is afraid of anything to do with bed and the dark? If a child has been abused orally, wouldn't it resist putting anything in its mouth? A child complaining of pains in the tummy or pains "down below" might not be talking of physical hurt – indeed, there is often nothing to be seen – but of psychological hurt. Children do try and explain what's happening to them in the best way they can, but most of us adults are too stupid to hear what they're saying.'

If it does all come out into the open, either because the child discloses or someone stumbles across clear evidence, the reaction of people close to the child – most importantly, her parents if the abuser isn't her father or stepfather, or her mother if he is – is absolutely crucial in determining whether the damage can be healed or whether it is compounded. Many people working with abused children, and adults, believe that a negative reaction, whether it's refusing to believe the child, or blaming her for what has happened, can be almost as damaging as the abuse itself. Certainly, research done in the United States shows that if parents reacted well, believed the child when she told, supported her, told her immediately it wasn't her fault, then the damage could be minimized.

When Sue (see p. 36) was thirteen, it all came out. 'My stepfather had come into my bed one night and, as usual, I hadn't wanted to know. There'd been a struggle and in the process the locket my mum had given me got broken. He gave up and went back into their bedroom, but I followed him with the broken locket and his underpants which he'd left in my bed, and chucked them at him.

'I got dressed and was half-way down the stairs when mum appeared and said, "Hang on. I'm coming with you." Eventually, we wound up at the police station at 3 a.m. I made a statement – with difficulty; the policewoman kept stopping and asking me how to spell words like "masturbate". They then insisted on showing the statement to mum because I was under sixteen.

'At first she did believe me, but when we got home she asked him if it was true. He swore on his baby's life that he'd never touched me, and she believed him. That was that. The police said that as I had a boyfriend he would be blamed if I was found not to be a virgin, and it would probably be my best bet to drop the whole thing. So I did.

'For the next few years I was shunted round the family, propositioned in some houses, treated like a skivvy in others, and I never spent another Christmas or summer holiday with mum again. So when I was thirteen everything I'd ever wanted had been taken away from me.'

In Sue's case, even though she wasn't believed, disclosing did end the abuse. In other cases, where a child discloses and is not believed, the abuser has carte blanche to carry on abusing. And as Anne Bannister points out, it only adds to the child's suffering and anguish because it confirms what the abuser has probably told her all along: 'No one will believe you if you do tell,' or 'No one will do anything to stop it.'

One of Richard Johnson's sisters told their mother what was happening, but she didn't believe her. 'But when I told her what dad had been doing to me when I was ten she believed me, called the police, and he wound up going to prison. That's not uncommon – when boys disclose, mums usually believe them. The thinking must be, "Boys don't lie about things like that." But a lot of mums don't believe daughters – not the first time they disclose, anyway. As a result a lot of daughters hate their mothers as much as, if not more than, they hate the fathers who actually abused them. My sister certainly hated mum.'

If the abuse doesn't come to light, it sometimes ends when the child is physically and psychologically strong enough to stop it.

'When I was thirteen,' said Sally, 'my father got home drunk one night from an army "do", came into my room and tried to rape me. I said no, and that was it. He never tried anything again. I couldn't understand – and still can't – why I could say no then, and make it stop, but I couldn't earlier.'

For other children, even though the abuse has stopped, the possibility of it starting again hangs over their heads like an ominous black cloud. Although Sarah's father stopped taking her into his bed after she had threatened to tell her mother when she was seven, there were isolated incidents throughout her childhood. He would touch her breasts and try to kiss her. 'I lived in a permanent state of terror that it was going to start all over again. When I contacted Incest Crisis Line initially, my first words were, "Mine's not a terribly serious case . . ." But the counsellor said that the constant dread I had lived with was devastating psychologically, and whereas he always knew exactly what was going to happen to him and that it would soon be over, I didn't.'

Sometimes the abuse ends when the child grows up and leaves home, but not always. Until last year, even though Kathy is now thirty and married for the second time, her father would come up behind her and push himself against her. 'I'd foolishly agreed to go on holiday with my husband and stepdaughter and my parents, and even before we got on the plane, he'd done it. He did it several times once we'd arrived until I turned on him and threatened to tell my mum if he didn't stop. It worked, but by then the holiday was ruined for me.'

Sarah was in her mid twenties and had been living with her boyfriend for four years when her father, by then a widower, turned up and said he had nowhere else to go. 'I said he could stay that night, and he tried to get into bed with me. Then in the morning I found him peeping at me through the bathroom keyhole. Just a few years ago, one of my brothers who lives abroad came home to see us, and we went to visit my father together. We were larking about on the doorstep, and my brother put his arm round me and gave me a hug. Just at that moment, my father opened the door, and the look on his face was pure sexual jealousy.'

LONG-TERM EFFECTS

Even if the abuse does stop, the problems it has caused don't go away, although many victims – and all too often the authorities – assume that they will. Rose is not untypical. 'Once my father had left, I thought, "That's that. Problem solved. Now we can relax." There was no point in telling my mum because it was past history. What you don't realize at ten is all the problems that will come out later when you're twenty or thirty.'

Anne felt exactly the same. When the photographic evidence of her abuse came to light, she was sent to see a psychiatrist. 'I was told it was either that or court. But I felt it was an utter waste of time. There was nothing wrong with me then. It was later that I got totally screwed up.'

Certainly if the victim has never told anyone about the abuse – or did pluck up the courage to tell at the time but was not believed or was blamed – the long-term effects can be crippling. The memories are buried very deeply, so deeply that many victims simply don't associate the problems they're having in adult life with their childhood experiences. 'It was simple,' said Sally. 'My life was a mess – I was promiscuous, I drank too much, even dabbled in drugs – because I was a horrible person and that was how horrible people behaved. The idea that it could be connected with what my father had done to me as a child never entered my head.'

Sexual abuse in childhood is at the root of many mental health problems. Community studies (that is, studies carried out in the general population, not among hospital patients or known victims) in the USA suggest that women who were sexually abused as children are twice as likely to suffer from depression, and to suffer more often and more seriously, needing more hospital treatment than their non-abused counterparts. In other similar sorts of community studies in the USA, it was found that, of the women who had been sexually abused as children, between 17 and 27 per cent had a history of alcoholism, compared with between 4 and 11 per cent of women who had not been abused. The figures for drug abuse ranged between 21 and 27 per cent for victims of sexual abuse and from 2 to 12 per cent for non-victims.

Many women have a very low opinion of themselves. In some cases, the abuse had been accompanied by constant verbal denigration. Tricia, who is now an office manager in London, was abused by her father from the age of eight, when her mother died, until she was fourteen. 'If I ever did well at anything, he'd say things like, "You think you're a fucking clever bitch, don't you?" and proceed to put me down. Until all that started I'd been a bright kid at school, but from then on it was downhill all the way. It was partly because I couldn't concentrate – my mind was so clouded with everything that was happening at home – but partly because I became afraid to succeed. That's still with me. I'll get so far with something, and if it's all going well I'll do something really stupid to check my progress. After all those years of being told what a load of rubbish I was, it's become inbuilt. I do it for myself.'

When Kathy (see p. 35) looks back at her life, she can see a pattern of lost, wasted or wrecked opportunities. 'I suppose I felt I couldn't succeed because I was no good, and didn't deserve anything nice happening to me. So I made sure I failed.' Her sense of worthlessness was reinforced when at the age of eighteen she felt she had to tell her mother what had happened. What prompted her disclosure was the discovery that her father had abused her seven-year-old niece, his granddaughter. 'My mum said, "Oh, he must have been drunk", but we both knew he was practically teetotal, so it wasn't that. But from then on it was brushed under the carpet. The fact that she chose to stay with him and so rejected me confirmed what I already believed – that I was absolutely filthy, guilty and worthless.'

In her late teens Sally went out with a man who had been a friend of the family and told him what had happened in her childhood. 'He just didn't believe me. He said I must have got hold of the wrong end of the stick, or misinterpreted my father's actions. That was absolutely devastating. I even began to doubt my own memory.'

Sarah grew up with no self-confidence whatsoever. She thought of herself as ugly, horrible and ill-natured, and always assumed that everyone else was better, cleverer and more admirable in every way than she was. 'For years I couldn't say if I didn't like something and I've never felt I was entitled to an opinion of my own. I was in a meeting very recently, and we were discussing a topic on which I do have very strong views. But I sat not saying anything until a colleague said, "You know, Sarah, you do have a right to an opinion!"'

Not surprisingly, many victims of child sexual abuse go on to develop sexual problems in adult life, which manifest themselves in a whole variety of ways. Some people find the whole idea of sexual relationships repellent and stay well clear. Two studies carried out in the USA both found that around 40 per cent of women who had been abused as children never married. Molly, who was abused by her brother for almost ten years, is not remotely interested in having a relationship with a man. 'I'm very much overweight because I don't want to attract men. I don't think that's something which is likely to change, either. I do have one friend who is male and we get on very well, but it is just a friendship; I certainly don't want it to develop into anything more.'

Incest Crisis Line counsellors find they get a lot of calls from young people of both sexes, who are concerned that their abuse experiences might have made them gay. For women, although those experiences may well give them an understandably jaundiced view of men, they don't challenge their basic sexual orientation. In the usual way of things, most girls would expect their sexual relationships to be with men. For boys who've been abused by men, though, there can be real problems. Many of them fear that they will become homosexual against their will, as though that particular sexual orientation was somehow infectious.

Mike (see p. 39) started going out with girls in his mid teens, mainly to convince himself that his experiences with his uncle hadn't made him homosexual. But later on it became clear that those experiences had affected him in another way. 'It wasn't until I got married and had to sleep with someone that I found I couldn't bear to be touched. That made it extremely difficult for me to make love to my wife, so she in turn thought I was very cold and unloving. I didn't connect what my uncle had done to me as a child with how I felt then – I thought it was just that I'd only ever slept alone in a single bed, and that I'd get used to sleeping with someone else.'

It was only after his uncle suddenly reappeared a few years ago, and as a result Mike had a series of mental breakdowns, that he was able to tell his wife. 'It is better now. I don't mind her touching me now, but if she catches me off guard, my instinct is still to freeze.'

According to psychotherapist Jenner Roth, one of the problems that beset many victims of sexual abuse in childhood is that they see any physical contact as sexual. 'We, in this culture, have real problems in differentiating between affection and sexuality anyway, and it gets people really messed up. Person A wants affection and the only way she knows how to get it is through sex, which is not satisfactory but gives her a bit of affection. Person B wants sex and thinks the way to get it is to give a bit of affection . . . The relationship is doomed. Certainly the difference between sex and affection is one of the basic things we work on when we're helping people with their sexuality.'

Many women who are married or in long-term relationships find sex difficult. One American study of incest survivors found that 80 per cent of them couldn't enjoy sex, couldn't relax.

'I can't bear to be controlled,' said Paula, 'and even though I don't really want to take control myself, it's the only way I can make it work. I can't even cuddle if I don't want to – not even with the children.'

For many victims, sexual abuse was a wholly painful, distressing, unpleasant experience. For others, though, sex was sometimes pleasurable, which creates powerful guilt feelings. 'I found it very, very hard to accept that I got pleasure from what my father did,' said Sally, 'or to forgive myself for it. I couldn't come to terms with the fact that something that was so clearly wrong could be so nice.'

That's a common reaction among victims. They feel that because they responded sexually, they must have wanted it to happen and therefore it must be their fault. What counselling can do is help them see that, to a degree, a sexual response to skilful masturbation is as much an involuntary physical reaction as laughing is to being tickled.

Other women, as a result of their experiences, become promiscuous. A series of American studies found that over a third of the victims interviewed could be described as promiscuous, though researcher David Finkelhor points out that this could be as much to do with the low self-image of the women questioned as with the actual number of partners.

But certainly many women describe themselves in that way. Anne describes periods in her life when she's gone on what she calls 'benders' – having several men in the course of an evening. 'I was taught from the very beginning that sex was what I was here for. My stepfather used to say while he was screwing me, "I'm teaching you now what you'll have to do when you're older. Men won't like you when you grow up if you don't know how to do these things." From about thirteen on, if anyone wanted to screw me, OK, fine. I didn't care. Sex was a way of getting what you wanted whether it was a bit of affection or a bed for the night.

'I liked one-night stands. You meet a bloke, go to bed and that's it. If you have a longer relationship with someone, it starts to get complicated. They'd want oral sex, and after my experiences as a child, it's something I just hate. The bloke would get upset because I didn't want to, make me feel guilty so I'd do it just for a quiet life, but afterwards I'd feel really resentful, and that would be the end of that.'

Sue's attitude to sex is what you might call a masculine one. 'It's like meat in the supermarket. "Oh, I fancy that bit. I'll have it." I can meet a bloke, have sex with him, get dressed and walk away without any feelings whatsoever. It's cold and hard and nasty, and not how it should be at all. But when your stepfather teaches you how to do it at eight years old – and even buys you a sex manual, for God's sake – it becomes a mechanical exercise.'

Although Sarah has never been promiscuous, she believes that as a result of her childhood experiences she can't relate to men other than in a sexual way. 'I still feel that I must convey through my eyes that I'm a tart. I'm still very uneasy around men, and try never to be alone with them. I can't have a natural, friendly relationship with a man.'

It's not just women who have been sexually abused in childhood who become promiscuous. Men do, too, though society usually takes a far less negative attitude to their behaviour.

Simon's (see p. 37) family and male friends have always thought he was jack-the-lad with a string of girlfriends, none of whom lasted very long. 'I've had over a hundred relationships, though a more accurate description might be "a plethora of penile stabbings".

'I have thought about it a lot and have had some counselling in the last year or so, and I can see now how the experiences I had at twelve with the housekeeper affected me. That relationship ended when my parents found out and warned her off, though – surprisingly – they didn't fire her. I knew nothing about it; as far as I was concerned, one minute she couldn't get enough of me, and the next it was all over. What I felt then was a mixture of lust and hate. I hated her and I was foul to her young child, but I'd pursue her sexually in the worst kind of male, animalistic way.

'By the time I was fourteen it had fizzled out, and I turned to younger women! It was extremely easy to get into bed with them – there was no mystery about it – and it never crossed my mind that you could have a relationship without sex. After all, that's what I'd learnt at twelve that relationships with women were about.

'And yet I also had a major problem with premature ejaculation, which resulted I suppose from the anxiety about my performance that had developed in my relationship with the housekeeper. So many of my relationships went from hot to cold, with sexual intercourse at the fulcrum, and someone I couldn't bear to be parted from for half an hour before, I suddenly couldn't face seeing again for a week. The exact nature of the problem became very clear a couple of years ago when I was seeing two women at the same time. One I was mad about sexually and there were no difficulties with premature ejaculation, but out of bed I just didn't want to spend time with her at all. With the other woman, although I loved her, enjoyed her company enormously, admired and respected her, I just couldn't get it together sexually.

'I find it damned nigh impossible to express love sexually. On the one hand there's "dirty lust" and on the other there is "clean pure love", and though I am working on it, bringing the two together is proving very hard.'

According to Dr Estela Welldon, psychiatrist and author of a new book, *Mother, Madonna, Whore. The Idealisation and Denigration of Motherhood* (Free Association Press, 1988), Simon's situation is common in Mediterranean countries. 'There, it still happens that the housekeeper or the maid initiates the young boys of the family into sexual activity. It's not so harmful for them because, having been brought up in the Catholic faith, in their minds the division of women into mothers – madonnas – and whores has already happened. It is difficult for them to have sex with mothers, even the mothers of their own children, so they look outside the family for it.'

As Simon's experience shows only too clearly, having sex constantly doesn't mean there is necessarily any pleasure in it. The same is true for women, though since theirs is the passive role, it's easier for them to hide the fact. Many switch off and feel nothing. Anne has even been known to read the paper while it's happening. Others begin to feel disgusted with themselves for being promiscuous and even if they have been able to forgive themselves for having been abused, they find it much harder to forgive the resulting promiscuity.

'Up to a year ago,' said Rose, 'I would have said, "I chose to behave like that. I was an adult, and free to make my own decisions and therefore I am responsible for the way I was." But I've done a lot of thinking, and now I don't see it like that any more. I believe that I was programmed as a child to be sexual, and while I wouldn't claim that everything that's happened in my life is a result of what my father did to me, I am convinced that my relationships with men have been directly influenced by those experiences.'

It is easy to see how victims of sexual abuse can drift into prostitution. As Anne puts it, 'You get so bloody angry about giving it away for nothing to people you don't care about, who give you all the lies under the sun, that you think you might as well go on the game.'

For boys who are abused, prostitution is also an easy trap to fall into. Nigel, who was anally raped with a bottle by a family 'friend' when he was twelve, worked as a prostitute until he was twenty-one. 'Most abusers are very clever. They will often give a victim sweets, or presents, or even cash, after they have abused him, making him feel that what happened was some kind of bargain between them or even that it was what the child wanted. It's easy to see how being rewarded for sexual favours can lead a child who has been made to feel worthless very naturally on to prostitution.'

After his father was imprisoned for physical abuse (the authorities chose not to prosecute him for sexual abuse), Richard Johnson, who was then twelve, became a prostitute in the King's Cross area. 'When you're working the streets, it's very easy to drift into petty crime. If a doddery old buffer came along to be serviced, you'd duff him up and steal his money. Then I stopped being a prostitute myself and became friends with a female prostitute who was much older than me. She not only taught me about heterosexuality but, more important, she taught me not to punish myself for what had happened. Unfortunately what she also did was make me very angry with society. She used to say, "They knew what was going on and they couldn't have cared less." If you feel that way about society, it's not a big step then to serious crime.'

As we have seen, some 40 per cent of prison inmates in the UK have been abused and Ray Wyre points out that, according to some studies, 75 per cent of all men in US prisons were sexually abused as children. 'People can't have betrayal experiences as children with no consequences.'

It is perhaps predictable that people who were sexually abused in childhood often find it very difficult to make successful relationships in later life. Some women choose, subconsciously, to marry men who will abuse them because that is a pattern with which they are familiar. Various community studies done in the USA indicate that, of women who were sexually abused as children, between 38 and 48 per cent married men who battered and/or sexually assaulted them, compared with 17 per cent of women who were not victims of sexual abuse in childhood.

Rose's husband battered her. 'Of course I didn't know when I married him that he would beat me, but my father, as well as sexually abusing me, used to beat my mother terribly; I suppose that on some deep level that's what I believed relationships were like, and I probably unconsciously picked up the same qualities my father had in my husband.' According to Anne Bannister, the mind's way of trying to heal itself is by repeating a trauma in order to make sense of it. 'It's as though the mind is saying, "It was my fault, but this time I'll handle it better. This time I'll get it right."'

That could also be an explanation for the fact that victims of child sexual abuse run a higher risk in adult life of being raped than women who were not abused as children. One study carried out in the USA in 1986 found that between 33 and 68 per cent of the sexual abuse victims questioned had been raped, compared with 17 per cent of the non-victims.

Other women whose trust has been destroyed, and who have been programmed to relate only sexually to men, find it very hard to relate to them in any other way. 'I've been going out with Bob for a year now,' said Anne, 'the longest I've ever been with one person in my life. For a long time he was just a mate, coming round to see me, and because I wasn't interested in him sexually it never crossed my mind that he might be a nice bloke to go out with. Then one night he kissed me, and of course I got him into bed. I knew what I was dealing with then, I thought, and started to treat him like I treated other blokes. I just didn't notice that what he wanted was a relationship with me. He has never ever let me down. He's always rung or come over when he said he would.

'One day I found this stray kitten and tried to rear it by hand, but it died on me. I rang him up to tell him, almost in tears, and that night he arrived with a big bunch of roses. That sort of thing doesn't happen to women like me. I have my dreams like everyone else, of getting married or at least settling down with someone for a very long time. No one wants to live on their own for ever. But people don't stay with people like me. We're difficult to live with. We don't just have bad days, we have bad weeks. We have times when we're so selfish, other times when we're so submissive. I try not to be, but it usually comes out then as aggression. I can't find a happy medium . . .

'I can't bring myself to tell Bob I love him, though I'm still not sure that I know the difference between sex and love. I used to say "I love you" to blokes all the time and it meant nothing. Now it does mean something, I can't say it.'

It took a while for Anne to pluck up the courage to tell Bob about her childhood. She had told a couple of other men whom she had cared about, and they had both left her. 'I felt I had to tell him or the relationship would go nowhere, but I also knew that if I did tell him there was a chance I'd lose him. We watched Roger Cook's programme about child pornography one night and he could see I was very upset. He asked, "Why are you so angry?" I told him, first of all about Tony and then later about my stepfather, though all I said was, "He messed around with me"; I didn't say, "He raped me", as I should have done. And then I waited for the phone call to say that he wouldn't be coming round any more, or for the phone calls to stop. But they didn't. A couple of months later, I told him I had been really worried about telling him because I was afraid that he'd leave. He asked for a cuddle then. He was really upset that I could even think that. But I still can't believe the relationship is going to last.'

Rose's marriage broke up, not because her husband was violent to her but because she discovered that he had been sexually abusing her eight-year-old daughter from a previous relationship. All the memories of her own experiences with her father, which she had until then successfully buried, came flooding back, compounding the guilt she felt at having been unable to protect her daughter. During what was a fraught and difficult time she got a lot of support from a male friend, who could hardly have been more different from her husband or father – gentle, kind, caring. 'Eventually, over a year or so, it grew into something else. But then last year something in me snapped. I wanted no sex, I just wanted to be left alone. The psychologist who'd been helping my daughter saw the two of us together and was appalled at how cold I was to him. She said, "You've got so much going for you . . ." I spent the weekend alone and really thought hard about myself and my feelings towards him.

'Gradually I understood. I don't allow men to come close emotionally. Sex is no problem, but emotionally, it's so far and no further. I couldn't run the risk of making myself vulnerable to another man who would abuse me. Now I know that and have begun to face up to it, I can start doing something about it, I hope . . .'

Psychotherapist Jenner Roth finds that many people come to her because they have great difficulty in forming stable relationships. 'In the course of eliciting information about their past, I find they will often say, "Oh yes, I was sexually abused as a child, but that was a long time ago. Forget about that . . ." They have never been able to deal with the abuse, and don't see the link between it and their present difficulties.

'One of the consistent patterns in adults who were sexually abused as children is isolation, the inability to develop intimacy.

They learn to isolate themselves in order to deal with the abuse, and to survive. It can't be talked about because with serious sexual abuse there is always a threat – covert or overt – that it must not be exposed. And that is a very difficult pattern of behaviour to un-learn because there is no trust anywhere, so how can you develop an intimate relationship which assumes trust, where you can share, and are not threatened?'

When a child is sexually abused by her father or stepfather, she is not only damaged by the abuse itself but also by the loss of normal parenting that inevitably results. Many victims feel that loss keenly in adult life. 'I would so love to have a dad,' said Paula, now in her thirties, 'a real, proper dad, because deep down I'm a very cuddly, loving, affectionate person and I never had the chance to show all that. My mother was very cold and unaffectionate, so I feel I really need both a mum and a dad. I did actually ask my husband last year if he thought there was any way someone my age could find foster parents!'

Kathy, too, still grieves for the loss of a father, though she didn't realize just how much until she married for the second time. 'My husband was divorced and had custody of his six-year-old daughter, so obviously she came to live with us when we got married. I was insanely jealous of her to start with, jealous of the close, loving, normal father–daughter relationship she had with her dad, and of the fact that she was having a "proper" childhood. I was a total bitch to both of them for the first couple of years, so much so that the marriage almost broke up. It was only when I finally got up enough courage – out of a bottle – to tell my husband what had happened to me as a child that things started to improve. He believed me totally, and said, "Thank God that's all it is. I thought you'd gone mental!" Since then he has been a tremendous support and I have a very good, close relationship with my stepdaughter. I have told my husband that if he ever lays a finger on her, I'll kill him. And I mean it.'

Other women try to replace the 'real' father they never had by choosing a father figure as a husband. Sarah's husband is strong and very protective of her, something her father finds hard to accept. 'He has often said he doesn't like the way my husband treats me, and one day he actually said, "You married a father, not a husband." It was on the tip of my tongue to say, "How would I know? I don't know what a father is!", but I didn't.'

Sally realizes now that her main reason for marrying her husband, who was gentle, kind and solid, was because she wanted someone to look after her in the way her father should have done but didn't. 'I felt I was the weak one in the marriage, a passenger who had no rights – just like a child, in fact. In the last year my life has undergone a transformation. I have confronted my father with what he did to me; I've come to understand that what happened was in no way my fault. I'm even beginning to forgive myself for the promiscuity in my teens that resulted. I feel I am a very different person now, and that person needs an equal relationship, not an unequal one. Before I finally decided to separate from my husband we went to Marriage Guidance, and the counsellor said it seemed that I felt I had now grown up and was finally ready to leave home. She was dead right. That's exactly how I felt.'

THE PROBLEMS OF PARENTHOOD

Being a good parent is something people learn mainly from experience. For children who haven't experienced it, it is much harder, though by no means impossible, to become good parents themselves. Valerie Howarth, Director of ChildLine, finds that many of the adults who ring are worried about their relationship with their children. 'It's not that they are afraid they're going to abuse them. It's more that they feel cold, distant, unable to respond properly. They're frightened of over-responding, and of what happened to them happening to their children.'

In Sue's case, she knows she is unreasonably protective of her three children, and particularly her daughter now that she's reaching the age Sue was when her stepfather started abusing her. 'I can't let her out of my sight. There's a school journey coming up and I don't want to let her go. If she sits on anyone's lap, I can't take my eyes off her. I want her to have everything that I never had – the chance to grow up slowly, to have a normal childhood. I'm not quite as bad with the boys, because I wasn't a boy I suppose, but I'm still over-protective of them. I know they are suffering, and that I'm stopping them from being proper children. Maybe because I've been so strict with them they'll be really lax with their own kids, and who knows what might happen to them. It's a vicious circle and it all stems from that one evil bastard . . .'

Anne, too, above all else wants her five-year-old son to have a normal childhood, but it's very hard. 'You want to make sure they can be children for as long as possible, but at the same time you're contradicting that. Because kids are so trusting, you know how vulnerable they are, so you have to teach them to trust no one and that means they're not proper kids any more. When they're watchful, on the defensive, they don't even look like children should.'

In the course of her work, Jenner Roth sees another danger faced by parents who have not been able to deal with their own experiences of abuse in childhood. 'The effects can be perpetuated in the next generation in a variety of ways. In one scenario, the parent says, "I was abused and therefore anything sexual is bad, including my own children's natural sexual development, so I will tell them they are filthy and disgusting." They in turn will have enormous difficulties with their own sexuality and may become victims of various forms of sexual abuse.'

There does seem to be some evidence to support that view. One US study found that 24 per cent of mothers of sexually abused children were themselves incest victims, compared with only 3 per cent in a non-abused control group. One possible explanation the researchers offer is that when closeness and affection have a sexual meaning for the mother as the result of her own experiences as a child, she then keeps her distance from the child, both emotionally and physically, and as David Finkelhor's work demonstrates, that is a factor in creating a situation which allows – not causes – sexual abuse to happen.

Child psychiatrist Eileen Vizard's job is to work with children, not with adult victims. 'But so many of the mothers of these children are actually victims themselves that you end up doing counselling work with adult victims anyway.'

Anne Bannister of the NSPCC in Manchester first started working with child sexual abuse victims because when she was working with mothers who had physically abused their children, she found that almost three-quarters of the mothers themselves had been sexually abused as children. But as psychologist Gerrilyn Smith is quick to point out, that is not to say the reverse is true, and that all women who were abused will be unable to protect their own children from abuse. 'In fact, most of them go on to protect their own children very successfully and for that reason they never come to the attention of the authorities. It's only those who *don't* succeed that do.'

Anne Bannister points to Nicholas Groth's work in the USA with male sex abusers; Groth found that between 40 and 50 per cent of them had been sexually abused as children, and 80 per cent had been physically abused. 'It's been said that children react in three main ways to abuse. First, they can say to themselves, "I have become victimized and I will continue to be a victim throughout my life." Or, secondly, they can say, "I will not be a victim again, and since life obviously consists of abusers and victims, I will be an abuser." Or, thirdly, they can say, "I can integrate this experience along with other experiences I have had and I will be neither of those things." It's mainly women who choose the first route because I think females feel subconsciously that the victim role is the female role, and to be otherwise is unfeminine.

'Fortunately those who choose the second route are in the minority, and though there are women who abuse sexually, abusers tend to be male. They choose that route because they learn through socialization, very early on, that they are the ones with the power in this society and therefore the male role is not a victim role.'

For that reason some boys find the fact that they were forced into the role of victim so deeply disturbing that they react with aggression and violence. Meg's twelve-year-old son, Christopher, was sexually abused eighteen months ago by the parish priest who had also become a family friend. 'His personality has changed completely since then. He is violent – always getting into fights at school, aggressive at home. He smashed the ghetto-blaster we bought him, and when we replaced it, he smashed that one too, and he's ripped all the posters he used to treasure off the walls. We all go in fear of his temper.'

Christopher has been seeing a psychiatrist, but he still finds it too painful to talk about what happened; the psychiatrist doesn't really see how he can help him further until he can. But at least in Christopher's case, the abuse is out in the open and there is help available.

It seems likely that even fewer boys than girls disclose abuse – as we have seen, the victim role is not one that sits easily on male shoulders. Given that men tend to direct their bottled-up anger outwards towards other people, whereas women tend to direct it inwards, resulting in depression, suicide attempts and self-harm, the possible consequences are frightening.

According to Ray Wyre, 76 per cent of sadistic rapists were sexually abused as children. Child sexual abuse can also have other potentially lethal consequences. There is evidence to suggest that some of the men involved in seemingly motiveless mass killings – sniper incidents – in the USA in recent years were victims of sexual abuse, and in one case, the sniper himself was also an abuser.

In the first half of 1987, Incest Crisis Line received a number of calls from a young man named Michael who lived in Hungerford. He had been sexually abused as a child and was obviously very disturbed. The counsellors concerned are convinced that the caller was Michael Ryan, since the last call from Michael was a couple of months before the Hungerford massacre and it was too much of a coincidence for it to be otherwise. Normally ICL's calls are completely confidential, but in this instance they felt it was very important to let people know just how dreadful the consequences of abuse can be and how essential it is that victims should be helped.

Psychiatrist Dr Estela Welldon would not be at all surprised if that were the case. 'Where men have been involved in incestuous relationships, particularly with their mothers, it often comes to light in a very dramatic way – either in sadistic situations with other women, or in an explosion of violence.'

At the end of such a catalogue of misery and pain, it is all too easy to sink into pessimism. But people like Richard Johnson, Ray Wyre and Anne Bannister who are working with the victims of abuse, children and adults, don't believe they are all inevitably and irreparably damaged by the experience, doomed to become victims over and over again throughout their lives or to become abusers themselves.

As Richard Johnson says, there is a third option. 'You can become the person you would have been if you'd been left alone to develop normally. It's always there inside you, fighting to get out, and, with help, it can.'

3 Abusers

The response of most people to men who sexually abuse children is one of such revulsion that it rarely goes beyond 'Castrate them all', or 'Lock them up and throw away the key.' Those who are caught are pilloried by the press – 'monsters' is one of the favourite tabloid terms – and it's a well-known fact that 'nonces', as they're called by fellow inmates, are considered the lowest of the low by other prisoners and are often attacked by them. For that reason they usually spend their sentences on 'Rule 43' – segregated for their own protection.

But the fact that there are so many abusers who are never caught (and so many children damaged by their activities) means that we can't afford simply to dismiss them as freaks of nature and leave it at that. We have to confront the real possibility that someone known to us sexually abuses children, someone 'respectable', someone who seems nice, someone we couldn't possibly believe would do such a thing. That, of course, is what makes them so dangerous. If all child abusers had shifty eyes, greasy hair and dirty raincoats, protecting children would be a relatively simple matter.

Many people, especially victims of abuse, become extremely angry at the suggestion that money and skills should be devoted to the treatment of offenders. But for the protection of children, if for no other reason, we have to try and understand why abusers do what they do and therefore how they can be stopped – not just in the hope that individuals can be successfully treated and so prevented from abusing other children, but in the wider context of collecting information about how these men operate. Ray Wyre, a former probation officer and now a freelance counsellor and consultant, has had ten years' experience of working with sex offenders. 'People often find it difficult to understand why I do what I do, but one of the main reasons is for the information I get. A lot of work has been done on child protection, but the one thing I found no one had bothered to do was talk to the guys who abused children. That seemed crazy to me. They were the ones doing it, and getting away with it in many cases for years and years, so they were the ones with the information.'

In recent years, there has been some debate about the differences, if any, between those who abuse children within their own family – incest offenders – and those who abuse other people's children – paedophiles, men who are sexually aroused by children, boys and girls, under the age of puberty.

As Dr Eileen Vizard puts it: 'It was thought at one time that you had your paedophiles over here doing generally pretty harmless things, although among them you had the crazed killers that the tabloids seem to dig up regularly, while over there you had your harmless incest offender who was just an inadequate married man.

'Now we are seeing much more blurring of the boundaries. We don't really know, for example, because we haven't been asking the right questions, how many incest offenders have a hobby of paedophilia. We tend to assume that it's bad enough that they've done it with the family, and forget to ask about any outside activities.

'Just as worrying is the fact that most paedophiles are married men, and many of them have families. Those who aren't married still come from families, of course, and have brothers, sisters, nephews, nieces, and so on . . .'

In his work, Ray Wyre has come across paedophiles who have married either to try and overcome their predilection, or quite calculatingly in order to have children of their own. One man married three times, had three families, and committed incest with one child in each. Between marriages, he sexually abused other people's little girls. More common are the paedophiles who deliberately target single-parent families and move in with the mother, primarily to have easy access to the children.

Bill is a case in point. He is now in his late sixties, a white-haired, avuncular, rather quiet man. He started abusing children when he was seventeen, and only stopped when he was caught for the first time at the age of sixty-five. 'Some years ago, I placed an advert in the paper for a wife. I said I wanted an unmarried mother with a blue-eyed, fair-haired boy. I got eight replies. I chose one of them, but the boy was only six months old at the time, so of course I didn't commence straight away. I waited till he was six or seven . . .'

It's easy to see why Bill would have been considered a good catch, especially to a woman who had been let down by a man, rejected, and maybe even battered too. He is kind, gentle, non-threatening sexually – to an adult woman, anyway – and, of course, very keen on children.

A number of studies have been carried out, mostly in the USA, on sexual arousal to children, which show that paedophiles have a much greater penile response to slides of children than do either homosexual or heterosexual males. There have been very few studies on the responses of incest offenders. One of these involved playing audio tapes of sexual encounters with young girls to both incest offenders and paedophiles whose preference was for girls. It was found that the men in both groups developed 'significant erections' even though the girls in question were not the daughters or stepdaughters of the incest offenders.

PAEDOPHILES

Over the years, a number of psychiatrists and therapists have described distinct types of paedophiles, but Ray Wyre's categories seem particularly useful.

The first group he calls 'paraphiles'. 'Basically they would abuse anyone – children, old people, handicapped people. They are amoral or at least morally indiscriminate. One man I know of, who's now in prison serving a long sentence, performed many bizarre and aggressive sexual acts. He made peepholes in bedroom and bathroom walls. He got his wife to sleep with their son. He had sex regularly with his daughter from the age of eight, and also took her round to other child molesters and charged them for having sex with her. He would also get her to give him oral sex while she was having sexual intercourse with these other men. He also collected pornography – sadomasochistic magazines and child pornography – and was heavily into the occult.'

Paula (see p. 36) thinks her father falls into this category, though his behaviour wasn't quite so flagrant. Not only did he abuse her from the age of nine and quite blatantly fondle her mother sexually in front of the children, but she also discovered later that he was into other kinds of deviant sexual behaviour. 'Lots of other women, group sex, and apart from my own daughter, I believe he abuses children outside the family too.'

The second category are fixated paedophiles, men who are primarily interested in and sexually aroused by children under the age of puberty. They are usually interested in a very specific age group from the age of four to six, say, or six to eight, or eight to ten, and though they talk endlessly about 'loving' children, respecting them and caring for them, and deny that they do them any harm, once the object of their attentions has outgrown the age group he or she is usually ruthlessly dropped and a new child courted. In cases where they are interested in very young children, the child's gender is unimportant and they will abuse both boys and girls. With older children, the gender does matter and fixated paedophiles choose one or the other – usually boys, but not always.

On the whole, they are 'nice' men, respectable, often in good jobs, who show a 'kindly' interest in children, knowing how to talk to them and, almost more important, knowing how to listen, cultivating their friendship – and their parents' friendship.

That is exactly what happened in the case of Meg's son Christopher, whose experiences were described in Chapter 2 (see p. 58). With hindsight, she now realizes the priest quite deliberately courted the boy over a period of months. 'He'd come over to the house and spend hours with Chris up in his room, working on his computer. We thought of him as a family friend – I even bought him a Christmas present. Then he began inviting Chris over to his house and helped him with his homework. We were delighted, of course, that he took such an interest in Chris . . .'

One counsellor, Peter Righton, who has counselled a number of paedophiles, actually checked with the children involved in fourteen cases that the relationship was a 'real' relationship, as the paedophile had claimed. Only one boy failed to confirm the substance of what the paedophile had claimed. In *Perspectives on Paedophilia*, edited by Brian Taylor (Batsford, 1981), Peter Righton comments:

> Indeed the most common as well as the most poignant feature of the boys' tribute was that this particular friendship was

the first occasion on which the boy had felt himself fully accepted as a person in his own right. It was true that most boys claimed to be on distant or hostile terms with their parents, but the point seems to me to make a significant and sad comment on the social situation of some children.

Certainly paedophiles have a sixth sense which enables them to recognize children who are neglected or who are having problems at home, and to whom the offer of affection and attention is irresistible.

If these nice, respectable paedophiles are actually caught abusing a child, which they seldom are, they will claim it's a one-off, and can usually produce very impressive character witnesses to say that such behaviour is completely out of character.

Bill was arrested for abusing an eight-year-old girl in 1986, when he was sixty-five (see p. 61). He claimed that it had never happened before, that he didn't know what had come over him, and produced two magistrates as character witnesses to support his defence. In fact Bill had abused nearly *two hundred* children since he had started at seventeen. They included his stepson, four adopted children, and two others who were not officially adopted but who lived with the family permanently. He was also on the books of several different fostering agencies for many years, and though he can't remember exactly how many of the foster children he abused, he thinks it must have been over a hundred. The one child he says he never touched was his own natural son. 'I never wanted to. I could lie in bed with him and one of the foster children, and be aroused by the foster child, but not by my own boy.'

Bill was mainly interested in boys – in fact he used to ask the fostering agencies to send him boys – but he also abused girls. 'One in particular I remember got me aroused because she'd been next door and the bloke there had interfered with her. She told me what he'd done to her and I found that very exciting.

'It was a similar thing with the girl I got caught with.' (Not a foster child, incidentally, but one of her friends.) 'I used to get her to tell me about other blokes and what they did to her. She'd frig herself and so would I. I suppose the fact that I got aroused by hearing about what men did was my own homosexuality coming out. I had intercourse with the boys, if you can call it that, but not with the girls.'

It seems extraordinary that someone like Bill can abuse so many children over a period of nearly fifty years without any of the fostering agencies suspecting, or any of the children concerned saying anything to anyone in authority. What makes it even more strange is that his predilections were so well known among the children in the area that he was nicknamed 'Bent Bill'.

According to Ray Wyre, men like Bill get away with it for a variety of reasons. 'First they shift the blame on to the child. If you listen to them talking about children, you'll hear them say things like "They attracted me", "She wanted me to go the whole hog." Not only do they believe it, but the child believes it as well. Or they'll tell a boy it's a perfectly normal homosexual phase. If the guy uses a seductive approach, gradually wooing the child step by step, then with a boy of nine or ten, say, it's 95 per cent certain that he won't tell because he'll feel trapped by fear and embarrassment. Sometimes the guy will use threats, though these tend to be manipulative rather than threats of violence. One man told a child, "If you tell, no one will ever be able to cuddle you again."'

Ray Wyre describes in detail a typical cycle of behaviour which fixated paedophiles (who haven't managed to arrange a steady supply of children to their homes, as Bill did) often follow. It starts with fantasies and masturbation about previous sexual encounters, and those to come. The paedophile then gets to know a boy casually either in the street or somewhere children are known to gather. Bill used to favour the second row at a football match because the boys stand at the front, and if he stood just behind them it was easy to strike up a conversation. Amusement arcades, anywhere where there are video games, funfairs, particular local cafés, are all locations known to paedophiles.

The man gets to know the boy and his parents to establish trust, and takes him on outings. In the next phase, he persuades the boy to confide any problems at home or at school, and adopts a 'counsellor' role. In the final phase, he invites the boy to his home, encouraging him to tell his parents, and watches television or plays a board game with him. Very gradually he will start to touch the boy – an arm around his shoulders when he's arriving or leaving, say, or even a bit of mock wrestling. He may start to leave his arm around the boy for a bit longer. If the boy resists, then he'll move his arm and try again a few meetings later. Once the boy doesn't pull away when he puts his arms around his shoulders, he may touch his genitals through his clothing. If the boy resists, he'll stop and try again later. If he doesn't, he will move on to touching his unclothed genitals, to mutual masturbation, mutual oral sex and then buggery, first of the boy and then by the boy. Although boys are the usual targets for fixated paedophiles, sometimes girls can be too. One man, recently convicted, described an almost classic cycle of behaviour to Ray Wyre in which he lured girls into his home with the promise of playing Atari computer games and, starting with 'accidental' touching, moved gradually on to sexual intercourse.

'Just as heterosexuals plan their social and sex life,' said Ray Wyre, 'so do paedophiles. They plan in very great detail. If their behaviour was spur-of-the-moment, then paedophiles would be caught much more often than they are.

'Bill is not untypical. A new member joined our therapy group this week, who had been convicted of offences against two children, and at first he insisted that was all he'd done. But gradually, we got the truth out of him; along with two other men in a sex ring, he has molested approximately 1,000 children throughout his life.

'What they do is set up a whole pattern of behaviour, the various elements of which taken in isolation appear quite harmless, and so it goes largely unnoticed.'

Ray Wyre finds it strange that society feels it is safer to think of this kind of behaviour as impulsive, out of control, rather than as part of a familiar and therefore predictable cycle. 'If you accept that it's the latter, at least there's a chance of doing something about it, of helping the guy to recognize what's going on and to break the cycle himself. If it really was totally "spur-of-the-moment" stuff, then you haven't got a hope in hell of stopping it.'

This type of paedophile uses child erotica – even something as harmless as a Mothercare catalogue, or a holiday brochure, or even children's television programmes, can come into this category – as well as child pornography for masturbation, and for breaking down the inhibitions of the children who are his targets. Sometimes he will produce his own pornographic photographs or videos, either for himself or to exchange with or sell to other paedophiles. The invention of Polaroid cameras and, later, home video, neither of which involves outside processing, has been a boon to child pornographers, and home-produced, as well as professionally produced, pornography is an extremely lucrative international business.

Some people take the view that child pornography could provide a safety valve in that it may satisfy the urges of some paedophiles so that they don't need to abuse children. But as Ray Wyre points out, child pornography is *always* the record of a child being sexually abused and from that point of view alone is always harmful.

As for its effect on abusers, he finds that, for the vast majority of them, masturbation and fantasizing are a crucial part of their cycle of offending and of reinforcing their sexual orientation, and pornography plays an important part in that. 'I am not saying that child pornography makes men into sex offenders. There are men who would never, ever, sexually abuse children, no matter what stimuli they were exposed to. Equally, there are men who will abuse children anyway, whether they look at pornography or not. But in the middle there is a grey area where men could be influenced one way or the other, and even the slightest shift in the wrong direction could produce a lot more abusers.'

Joan Court, an extremely experienced independent social worker, has been appointed as guardian *ad litem* to represent the child's interests in a number of court cases where child sexual abuse was suspected. 'Almost all of them involved hard-core pornographic videos. I think a lot of adults do have sexual fantasies about children, and the videos break down the barriers between fantasy and acting out.'

Peter was convicted of sexually abusing teenage girls. 'I watched porno films for a long time before I started abusing, and I honestly believe it did have an effect on the behaviour I got into.'

Part of the appeal of child pornography for paedophiles is that it helps to 'normalize' what they do. Seeing lots of other people having sex with children means that they're not freaks. 'A lot of child pornography these days,' said Ray Wyre, 'is of children with children. To a paedophile that shows it's all very natural and "normal", the kids are enjoying it, so what they do to them is all right too.'

For the same reason, some paedophiles belong to organizations which actively promote 'consenting' sex with children, arguing that it does them no harm, and which campaign for the lowering of the age of consent. As one letter to the magazine produced by the Paedophile Information Exchange (PIE) put it, 'I am just as much against the child molester as any other person would be. But man–boy love, well, for me that's something sacred, and an agreement between two people who respect each other's freedom and right to do what they wish.' The writer of the letter felt that boys from about eight upwards were sufficiently 'sexually aware and responsible' to make those decisions.

Since the imprisonment of some members of PIE in this country a few years ago the organization has officially disbanded, but in fact it has just gone underground. Most of the other organizations are in the USA. There is the North American Man Boy Love Association, the Lewis Carroll Collector's Guild, Minor Problems, and the notorious René Guyon Society, whose slogan is 'Sex before eight or else it's too late'.

Paedophiles in this country are less openly organized. They tend to rely instead on electronic bulletin boards which can only be accessed by people with the right computer security code to exchange information on children. They are also sometimes involved in sex rings in which large numbers of children are passed around between abusers. One such that Ray Wyre uncovered in the Portsmouth area involved over 1,000 children. In a study carried out in Leeds in 1985 by Dr Nicholas Wild, it was found that a quarter of the girls diagnosed by paediatricians as having been sexually abused had been involved in sex rings, usually as ringleaders. 'With the help of two or three deputies they had provided sexual favours for, and introduced younger girls to, the male abuser, usually for money. Several of the ringleaders were known to have been sexually abused in the home. Each sex ring contained an average of twenty girls, making this an important type of abuse that appears to be widespread.'

Dianne Core of Childwatch, the Hull-based charity for sexually abused children and their families, has discovered several rings in various parts of the country. 'On average those involved about 200 children each.'

A third group is made up of inadequate paedophiles who may be suffering from some kind of mental problem – mental handicap or senility, say – which means that they may have a mental age of about twelve. They are often withdrawn and insecure, and are seen as social misfits. They have great difficulty in forming relationships with adults, and see children as an available, non-threatening alternative.

The fourth group, inadequate fixated paedophiles, are probably closest to the old stereotype of a child molester. They are lonely and isolated, lacking the interpersonal skills even to make relationships with children, so they are likely to hang around schools, playgrounds or public lavatories and molest strangers or very young children known to them. They are likely to expose themselves to children, and make obscene suggestions either in person or on the telephone.

Keith falls into this last category. He is twenty-six, though he looks younger, and is shy and awkward. He is on probation for exposing himself to two children, though he admits to having done it over 100 times without being caught, mainly to young boys, though sometimes to girls. 'I started on the gay scene when I was sixteen, with an older man – I've never been interested in adult women, though I'd like to be. I don't really know why I switched to flashing at kids. I don't know what I get out of it, really. I get very depressed sometimes, go out drinking, and then I just have to do it.'

Ray Wyre believes that in some ways this is the hardest group to treat. 'Some will stop at flashing, but others will progress to other offences. You can't simply look at the offence and make judgements about how the behaviour will develop. You have to look at the character of the guy too. Someone like Keith who is motivated by anger – depression is very often anger turned inwards – could go any way.'

There is yet another group, known as 'regressed paedophiles'. These are men who are primarily aroused sexually by adult women, but whose interest in children develops later in life, often triggered by stress: marital problems, divorce, or the death or illness of their partner. A number of studies in the USA showed that some men began sexually abusing their own children, or other people's, during a period of marital stress. They usually target girls and treat them like adults, which makes sense because their primary sexual interest remains adult women.

Although the category of regressed paedophile is widely accepted, Ray Wyre has his doubts about its validity. 'I'm very aware that it can easily be used to excuse behaviour – you often hear it referred to in court. But as with fixated paedophiles who are accused of a "first offence", further questioning may reveal that arousal to children has been a problem for a man for many years; though he may have controlled these desires, it isn't safe to assume that he has not offended before.'

At first glance, Peter might seem to fit the description pretty well. He divorced his wife in 1975 and brought up his three daughters, then aged between 18 months and six, singlehanded. 'I was an engineer, but I had to give up work because I couldn't find a job to fit in with the demands of the family. Over the years I became increasingly isolated – I was something of a recluse at the end – and the girls were my life.

'As they grew up, they'd bring their friends to the house. Now I have a fetish, which is being tickled, and I found that being tickled by these girls, who were between twelve and sixteen, turned me on sexually, so I actively encouraged them to do it. One thing led to another – to masturbation and oral sex with the younger girls, and full intercourse with the sixteen-year-olds. During these sessions, I used to switch on a video camera, and tape them for my own use. Initially the girls would only come to the house once a week or so, so I'd replay the videos and masturbate to them during the rest of the week. Later on, there were so many girls coming round all the time that I didn't need the video tapes myself. I started hiring them out at £3 a night, or selling them as master tapes to other people for anything up to £600.

'As for my own daughters, they didn't even know what was going on. Once they'd gone to school the other girls would bunk off, come round to the house, and be gone before my daughters got home from school.'

Ray Wyre wouldn't describe Peter as a paedophile, regressed or otherwise. 'He isn't turned on by pre-pubertal children. Many men are turned on by pubescent schoolgirls – you only have to look at the pictures of women dressed as schoolgirls in men's magazines to see that – but with most men, other mechanisms come into operation and prevent them from actually becoming abusers.'

Peter is also an incest offender. He denies ever having abused his own daughters, because he finds it too painful even now to face up to the reality of what he's done, yet he was charged with, and pleaded guilty to, incest with his youngest daughter who is still in care.

INCEST

Peter is a clear example of the blurring of boundaries between incest offenders and paedophiles. Many other incest offenders, though, tend to remain exclusively within the family, and often abuse only one child.

Sarah knows her father didn't abuse any of her five brothers and sisters. 'He was in love with me, obsessed with me anyway, and seemed to look to me for love and assurance. His own mother had put all her love and energy into his younger brother and he didn't get much of either from my mother. She was a very strong woman, and quite violent with him sometimes. He was terrified of her. I suppose I can understand why he did what he did to me, but that doesn't excuse it.'

Ken was imprisoned for incest with his daughter Cindy when she was between fourteen and sixteen, and is now living at home again with his wife and three children. 'What happened with Cindy was just falling in love, wanting to buy her presents, wanting to be with her . . . It's like you turn round one day and see something for the first time, even though it's always been there, and it hits you between the eyes. There's a feeling that she's yours, and too good for anyone else. I'd found her very attractive for some time, and got tremendously hurt by the things she told me about what boys at school had been doing to her. In my mind, she was a child that needed protection from other people. Unfortunately I put myself in their stead. It was as though I was saying, "Instead of being hurt by the outside world, come to me and whatever you need will be there. If you need sex, come to me rather than to these strangers."

'It started with cuddles, her sitting on my lap, and then when I'd go to get changed she'd be looking round the bedroom door at me. I started thinking about her as a woman instead of a child and a daughter. Once that boundary between parent and child breaks down and you feel it's a relationship between equals, I think it's inevitable that things will go badly wrong. We were on the edge for a while, and then one day we reached a point where I don't know whether I couldn't or just didn't stop myself and I went the whole way. I lost control, if you like.'

Ken still doesn't really understand why it happened. There weren't any real problems in the marriage – he still had a good sexual relationship with his wife – and he wasn't under any stress. 'It was more an attraction than anything else. It's very difficult to try and make people understand. If you genuinely accept responsibility for what you've done, you can't explain fully even to yourself why you did it. If you don't fully accept responsibility, then you'll always be convinced that you did it because she wanted you to. I mean, the question of Cindy ever refusing never arose. The number of times she asked me to go upstairs was unbelievable.

'In a way, when it gets to that stage you realize how wrong it is. You've got a situation where the person you should love and care for is behaving in a perverted manner and it's all your fault. I still haven't sorted it out. It's like I went through some great illness for two and a half years or I was an addict. Every time was going to be the last, but it never was. I knew I couldn't stop it myself. I knew I had to be stopped.'

MOTIVES

But for many incest offenders, abuse isn't about sex, it's about power. Richard Johnson and his twelve brothers and sisters were all abused anally, vaginally and orally by their father. 'In our house there was almost a bus-stop system, where he would penetrate seven or eight children one after the other while the rest waited their turn and had to witness what was going on. Sometimes he would take on four or five at the same time. It wasn't "sex" he was looking for. No one could climax with eight kids one after the other; no one is that potent. You could see he got his kicks out of dominating us kids, from the feeling of sheer power and the belief that he could do exactly what he liked with us.

'In my work with Incest Crisis Line, I often find that abusers on a power trip are people who are already in positions of power. I work a lot with policemen's kids, prison officers' kids, servicemen's kids . . . I'd say as many as 60 per cent of abusers are in positions of power or authority – as well as those I've mentioned, there are doctors, teachers, social workers, priests, and, yes, even scoutmasters.'

Gerrilyn Smith, a psychologist, also believes that the majority of abusers are 'power merchants'. 'And as power merchants they are extremely sensitive to power hierarchies. In my experience they will often be obsequious when in the presence of someone they perceive as more powerful than themselves, and a tyrant with someone they perceive as less powerful. It's very interesting as a woman working with male offenders. Though I have the professional power, they have the gender power and they're not quite sure how to play it. Sometimes the mask slips and they try and put me down very crudely because I'm a woman. Of course my male colleagues never see that and it's a very real clue to the nature of the man you're dealing with.'

Maria's father was in the army. 'He was basically a sadistic bully. He was violent to all of us all the time, and also when he was sexually abusing me. He wasn't happy unless he was hurting you. The more he hurt you the more he enjoyed it.'

Anger is another common motive for incest, according to Ray Wyre. 'The anger/conflict cycle is very common in relationships between stepfathers and stepchildren, and in some nuclear families. It starts with resentment – the child may resent the stepfather for taking the mother away and the stepfather may resent the child's refusal to accept him. If the man is insecure then he may need to cover up by establishing power. His expectations of the child are wholly unrealistic: he or she can do nothing right in his eyes, and it results in angry outbursts. If the child doesn't back off, the man sees the child as a threat to his masculinity and feels the need to put the child down. In some cases this can be by physical abuse, but in others, sex is seen as a way of punishing or humiliating the child. In one case the man said, "I told her so many times not to wear her pants in bed. We had an argument, so I ripped them off and had sex with her." It then became a regular occurrence.

'I am always a bit dubious about anger as a motive because an abuser can set up a cycle of behaviour where he knows he will become angry, and that gives him some justification for what he does.'

In other cases, the anger is directed not at the child, but at the mother, or even sometimes at women in general. Rose believes that was certainly one motive for her husband's abuse of her daughter, Tina. 'He knew he couldn't hurt me personally any more, but he knew that through Tina he could hurt me worse than anything. For the first five years of our marriage I had let my husband get away with murder – I put up with anything. But then he had an affair, and that changed things. I stopped letting him have his own way and started saying no. Although it turned out he had abused my daughter before then, it was after that time that it got much more serious.'

Sheila eventually came to realize that anger was the motive behind her husband Bob's abuse of her daughter (his stepdaughter) Angela, anger directed at his own mother and at herself.

'We live in a very small, remote community in Wales, and when I moved there with my first husband and the children, Bob and his parents were our next-door neighbours. Bob had always been dominated by his parents, his mother especially, and had never really been allowed to grow up. In order to escape from them as much as anything, he moved in with me and the children after my first husband died. I needed help desperately – I couldn't manage the farm by myself – but I couldn't accept Bob for himself. I saw him as a reincarnation of my first husband, and whenever he wanted to change things I'd say, "It was good enough for Philip, so it ought to be good enough for you."

'A couple of years after his abuse of Angela came to light we both had some very intensive therapy, and suddenly it all began to make sense. Bob was trying to assert himself against women who had bossed him around all his life. So what he had done was to pick on the only female in the family who didn't browbeat him, and dominate her. It wasn't lust, it certainly wasn't love – it was retaliation.'

In theory, child sexual abusers who are motivated by anger are thought to be a higher risk to children outside the family than seductive abusers like Ken. But Ray Wyre isn't so sure. 'The anger-motivated stepfather who is putting down his stepdaughter through sex is probably less dangerous to other children than a seductive guy, because his anger is to an extent created by and focused on that child – though of course it is in no way the child's fault. The seductive guy may well have a problem of sexual arousal to children, and probably won't stick at his own daughter.'

The key question to which everyone wants an answer, from victims trying to make sense of their experiences to professionals trying to prevent child sexual abuse, is: why do they do it? But as with all simple questions, the answer (if indeed there is an answer) is very complex. Over the years a number of theories based on psychoanalytic theory have been put forward, and more recently, theories on social learning and feminism. David Finkelhor, in his invaluable *Source Book on Child Sexual Abuse* (Sage, Beverly Hills and London, 1986), has divided them into four main categories.

The first group of theories explain why people's emotional needs might be met by sexual relationships with children; the second, why they would be blocked from finding both emotional and sexual gratification from adults; the third, why the usual social constraints and internal inhibitions don't prevent them from having sexual relationships with children; and finally, why they would find children sexually arousing. He himself takes the view that no 'single-factor theory' adequately explains why someone abuses children, but that it is always a combination of factors.

In the first category, there is the theory that abusers are themselves emotionally immature and therefore relate more easily to children than to their peers. Another theory linked with this suggests that it is not simply that they relate more easily to children, but that they have real problems in making relationships with adults because of their own low self-esteem. In relationships with children, they feel powerful, respected and in control. In a study carried out by Kevin Howells of Leicester University on a group of child sexual abusers, he found that one of the most important characteristics they pointed to in their choice of victims was lack of dominance.

A number of researchers have suggested that abusing children may be a way in which the abuser tries to master some trauma he suffered as a child – sexual or physical abuse, for example – by reversing the roles and becoming a powerful victimizer himself. But the whole issue of the impact of childhood abuse on those who become abusers themselves is a complicated one that will be dealt with later in this chapter.

Yet another theory on the emotional gratification that a man gets from sexually abusing children is that it is 'narcissism' – falling in love with the child he once was, or would have liked to be, and projecting that image on to other children. Perhaps if he was emotionally deprived as a child, in later life he tries to give the love he never had to a child who, in his mind, resembles himself. Obviously this theory only relates to men who sexually abuse boys, not girls.

There is certainly some overlap between these theories and those which explain why people sexually abuse children in terms of 'blockage' of the more usual, acceptable, emotional and sexual outlets. The blockage can be developmental – something has happened to prevent them from developing their adult sexuality. Some theories rely on Freud's Oedipus complex – abusers are thought to have such intense unresolved conflicts about their mothers that they can't relate to other adult women and so turn to children. Others see a disastrous first attempt at an adult sexual relationship as a possible reason.

Certainly a fear of sexual relationships with adult women seems common among both paedophiles and incest offenders. In one study using a well-known psychological technique, a picture of a semi-nude, mature woman was shown to members of both groups, and each man was asked to tell a story explaining the background to the picture – who the woman was, why she happened to be there, and so on. Instead of the sexual theme that heterosexual men usually produce, 85 per cent of the paedophiles and 87 per cent of the incest offenders came up with stories of her being ill, dying or dead.

The other sort of blockage is circumstantial. There are theories which hold that a man whose preference is for adult women, but whose marriage has broken down, for example, or whose wife is chronically ill or handicapped, may turn to children because that's all that is available. One study suggested that over 75 per cent of paedophiles are in fact 'regressed paedophiles'. But Ray Wyre, who doesn't accept that such a category exists, would argue that such men must already have a sexual arousal to children or they would find another sexual outlet. Certainly the majority of men in that situation either have affairs with adult women, use prostitutes, or even masturbate; they don't automatically start sexually abusing children.

But for some men, those alternatives may be blocked too by their repressive and, one has to say, rather distorted attitudes to sex.

Incest Crisis Line had a case recently of a Pakistani, who ran a restaurant in the Midlands, and who had sexually abused his daughter three times a week from the age of five until she blew the whistle on him when she was fifteen. To try and justify the abuse, he said he needed sex, couldn't get it from his wife and so had turned to his daughter. When he was asked why he hadn't taken a mistress or paid one of the many prostitutes working in the area where his restaurant was situated, he replied, shocked, 'Oh no! I couldn't do that. That's adultery!'

Another group of theories start from the premise that, since many men who may be sexually attracted to children, their own or other people's, are able to control those desires and don't go on to become abusers, there must be factors which break down the inhibitions of those who do.

One factor often cited is alcohol. Various American studies have shown that between 30 and 40 per cent of offences involved alcohol, that between 45 and 50 per cent of abusers have a drink problem. Keith, for example, who exposes himself to young children, has almost always been drinking before he commits an offence.

Other studies show that incest offenders use alcohol more than any other group. Jim, currently serving three years in prison for abusing his two stepdaughters, at the time aged thirteen and fifteen, had started drinking heavily because he was depressed as a result of unemployment. 'I even made my own beer and wine, and I was drinking a five-gallon barrel of beer and several bottles of wine every few days. It was at this stage that I started abusing my stepdaughters.'

But whether alcohol has a direct psychological effect on abusers' inhibitions in the way that it is supposed to for all of us, or whether it is a convenient excuse, isn't clear.

Another factor that reduces the usual inhibitions against sex with children in the family that has emerged in American studies is the presence of a stepfather rather than a natural father. In Diana Russell's 1986 community study in San Francisco, she found that of all the women who had had their biological father as a key figure in their lives from birth to the age of fourteen, one in forty-six (2.3 per cent) had been sexually abused by him. Of those who had a stepfather as the key figure, one in six (17 per cent) had been abused by him, and in those cases the abuse was generally more serious, with more sexual intercourse and more violence.

No similar community study has been carried out in this country. Great Ormond Street's study found that 46 per cent of the perpetrators referred to them were natural fathers and 27 per cent were stepfathers. The Child Sexual Abuse Unit in Manchester found roughly the same in their study. Forty per cent of abusers were natural fathers and 28 per cent father substitutes – stepfathers, adoptive fathers or mothers' cohabitees. ChildLine's figures showed that 50 per cent of female and 37 per cent of male sexual abuse victims were abused by their natural father, compared with 12 per cent and 3 per cent respectively by stepfathers. But what we don't know, because no figures have been published or even collected, is how many children in this country live with stepfathers as opposed to natural fathers, and therefore it's impossible to say what percentage of children in each category these figures represent.

One possible explanation for stepfathers abusing children is that they have no blood tie to the child, and therefore the taboo isn't as strong. And if they were not around during the child's early years, they would have missed out on the parent–child bonding that normally happens and so would feel less protective of the child in later years. (Certainly some doctors working in the field are hopeful that the much closer bonding between many young fathers today and their children may lead to a decrease in incestuous abuse in later years. But they are also aware that such increased closeness offers more opportunities for it . . .) There is, too, the very real possibility that the stepfather is a paedophile anyway and has married into the family primarily for access to the children.

The feminist viewpoint on child sexual abuse also falls into the 'disinhibition' category. It maintains that society, by its actions, does not really condemn child sexual abuse – the reluctance of the legal system in many countries to prosecute, for example, and the response of the authorities which seems to blame the child – and therefore, by default, condones it. As for incest, the feminist approach is that society sanctions men's belief that the family is their domain and that they are free to treat the women and children within it exactly as they please. Incest is not, therefore, an aberration, but merely patriarchal authority taken to excess. In instances where power and the need to dominate are the primary motivation that makes sense, but again, in most other cases a man must already have the desire to abuse a child sexually for the freedom to do so to make any difference.

So what is it that causes certain people to be sexually aroused by children? Ray Wyre is convinced that abusers learn their behaviour. He doesn't believe they are born that way. Something happens in childhood that affects their sexual orientation. 'Many fixated paedophiles, for example, had a sexual experience between about eight and twelve with a guy who was similar to what they have become. It's an experience they don't understand at the time, but it may be pleasurable and rewarding, not financially necessarily (though some paedophiles do give children presents and money), but in terms of attention. How many fathers are prepared to spend hours playing games with a boy or just talking to him? Later on in life, they repeat those experiences.'

A study carried out by Nicholas Groth in the USA found that many fixated paedophiles chose boys who were the same age they were when they were first abused, and committed the same kind of offence as that committed against them.

As a child Bill shared a bed with his uncle. 'When I was seven or eight he did the wrong thing to me, and though my grandmother moved me out when I said he wet the bed, he'd told his friends about me, and I kept bumping into people who wanted sexual services. Even when I started work at fourteen, one of the men there wanted me to go into the lavatory cubicle with him. Then, as I got a bit older, I started doing the same thing to young lads.'

Tom was first sentenced for raping a seven-year-old girl when he was nineteen, and is currently on probation under a treatment order for abusing a girl of thirteen and his own ten-year-old nephew. 'My parents put me into a children's home when I was five because I was uncontrollable. I was sexually assaulted there by members of the staff, and I fooled around with one of the girls who was about my own age.'

Another theory maintains that sexual arousal to children is the result of conditioning – an experience that is repeated so that it becomes imprinted. It may be a rewarding sexual experience with another child, so that the association of sex–child–pleasure becomes imprinted in a child's mind, or it can be an experience with an adult, in which case it is the relationship of child and adult which has the pleasurable connotations. For many people, though, such an experience in childhood is a one-off. For those who do go on to become abusers, the theory goes, the experience becomes the basis of fantasies used in masturbation, and it is known that masturbation is a very powerful means of reinforcing behaviour. Another possible explanation is that having witnessed adult sexual arousal to children, it is the most clearly defined model they have when they start to develop what David Finkelhor calls 'their own sexual script'. Certainly a number of studies carried out in the USA show that many abusers were themselves sexually or physically abused – sometimes both – during their own childhood.

Ken, for instance, was physically abused by his father as a child. 'When I was nine, I was sexually abused by a bloke I met. From then till I was sixteen I was abused lots of times, sometimes by force, and the bloke would give me money afterwards to shut me up. After my father had kicked me out at fourteen, I'd do it for money – to buy food or pay the rent. Then when I was sixteen I was frightened that I might become homosexual, so I went completely the other way and became rampantly hetero.'

One study in the USA of almost 200 abusers of girls showed that 10 per cent of them had had sexual contact in childhood with an adult woman (compared with only 1 per cent of the control group), while 18 per cent had had such contact with adult men (compared with 8 per cent of the control group). For abusers of boys, 33 per cent of them had had contact with adult men in their childhood. Other US studies have produced similar figures. In one group of 106 abusers, 32 per cent reported some 'sexual trauma' in childhood, compared with 3 per cent in a control group of policemen. Of that 32 per cent, over twice as many were fixated paedophiles than were regressed paedophiles. In a 1984 study of imprisoned abusers, Nicholas Groth found that over 80 per cent had suffered some kind of 'sexual trauma', though his definition was widened to include incidents such as witnessing sexual activity and being circumcised.

As for incest offenders, one study, again in the USA, found

that 21 per cent of them had been sexually abused before the age of twelve by an adult male, compared with 10 per cent of abusers of girls who were not related to them and 4 per cent of the control group. Another study, however, found considerably less sexual abuse in the childhoods of incest offenders than in those of other child abusers.

The research carried out at Great Ormond Street found that less than 10 per cent of the abusers (all abusing within the family, if not technically incest offenders) were reported initially by the professionals who referred them as having been sexually abused in childhood. During the course of treatment, though, others revealed that they had been sexually abused.

Richard Johnson finds that about 10 per cent of the abusers he confronts claim to have been sexually abused, although he would deny that this gives them an excuse to become abusers themselves.

Although Ray Wyre believes the figure for all offenders, inside and outside the family, who have been abused in childhood is much higher than 10 per cent, he shares Richard Johnson's view that it is no excuse. 'You can't allow abusers to use their past experiences to justify their present behaviour. In victim awareness sessions with my group, I use the members' own experiences to confront those guys who think their behaviour doesn't have any effect on their victims. But I always approach them as offenders first and victims second.'

Even if half, or only a quarter, of all child sexual abusers were abused themselves, it shows how vitally important it is for victims to be identified and treated as early as possible. Anne Bannister of the NSPCC and Greater Manchester Authorities Child Sexual Abuse Unit cites a case involving two brothers aged eight and ten. 'They have both been abused by their father – violent anal intercourse in conjunction with black magic. The eight-year-old is acting out – he's a naughty child, shouting, kicking other kids, saying sexually provocative things, looking up girls' skirts. *But* he is responding well to therapy and he is getting better. The ten-year-old isn't acting out at all. He's very contained, no problem at school, but he has started abusing other children in the children's home. If we're not very careful he will be a child sexual abuser because he's been so terribly abused himself and he's keeping so much of it inside. The older the child, the longer-term the abuse, the more difficult it is to treat.

Therapy works more quickly with younger children, because they have less to un-learn maybe.'

Although the cycle of abuse – abused children become adults who abuse children who become adults who ... – is obviously a cause for serious concern, it would be very dangerous to see it as inevitable. It is a source of great anxiety among the parents of victims and, as they grow older, of the victims themselves.

Mike (see p. 47) was abused by his uncle for six years, from the age of eight to fourteen, and his fears surfaced last year when his wife became pregnant. 'I kept on wondering if it was true that if you were abused, then you end up abusing kids yourself. If so, I felt perhaps I ought to leave my wife before the baby arrived because I can't bear to think of anyone having to go through what I did.'

There is also a danger in seeing abuse itself as the cause of abusing and looking no further for other explanations. If this were true, then why are at least 90 per cent of abusers male when at most only 35 to 40 per cent of victims are? There is no reason why the theory that victims take on the role of the victimizer in order to try and master the trauma they suffered in childhood shouldn't apply to women as well as men, but it doesn't seem to. It's more likely that the explanation for what is a near male monopoly in child sexual abuse lies in the differences between male and female sexuality. Men, for example, are brought up to expect to be the dominant partner, to have partners younger and smaller than themselves, and to be the initiators. Women, on the whole, still don't expect to be dominant; they expect their partners to be older and larger than themselves, and they don't expect to initiate a sexual relationship. Since children very rarely invite adults to have sex (unless, of course, they have already been abused), the situation doesn't arise.

As psychiatrist Dr Danya Glaser writes in her recent book (with Stephen Frosh), *Child Sexual Abuse* (Macmillan, 1988):

> Traditional 'masculinity' focuses on dominance and independence, an orientation to the world which is active and assertive, which valorizes competition and turns its face from intimacy, achieving esteem in the glorification of force. The fear at the heart of this image is of emotion ... The link between such a form of masculinity and sexual abuse is apparent; it is not just

present, but *inherent* in a mode of personality organization that rejects intimacy. Sex as triumph and achievement slides naturally into sex as rejection and degradation of the other.

Ray Wyre doesn't believe that sex offenders are a sub-species all on their own. He believes they are on the same continuum as all men – albeit at one extreme. 'I think the majority of men abuse women in some way, either by sexual harassment at work, innuendo, put-downs, swearing, and so on. In a sense all men are potential offenders – it's just that some of us are better at controlling our feelings than others – and that is something that all of us, and especially those men who are working with offenders, have to address.'

FEMALE ABUSERS

Although child sexual abusers are almost all men, there are some women who sexually abuse children. According to the official figures, the number of women abusers is very small. The Home Office criminal statistics for 1975–84 show that less than 1 per cent of offences were committed by women. The Great Ormond Street study found that 3 per cent of the abusers were women, 2 per cent acting alone and 1 per cent in conjunction with their partner. But given that official figures are known to be merely the tip of the iceberg, where women abusers are concerned it is likely that the under-reporting is even more marked than it is with male abusers.

According to psychiatrist Dr Estela Welldon, the reason is that motherhood is still sacrosanct, and women sexually abusing their children is still a taboo subject. 'People simply don't want to know. I see women who have been to all kinds of agencies to try and get help and they are simply not taken seriously. I even see it in my patient groups. When a man admits to the group that he has committed incest, everyone is very angry with him and shows hard feelings – a reflection of attitudes in society. When a woman says, always in a very tentative manner, that she has "funny feelings" about her daughter, wants to touch her sexually very much and so on, everyone in the group says, "Not to worry! It's just the maternal instinct. It's perfectly natural."

'It's also easier for mothers to get away with it. When a father becomes too intimate with a child, it can be seen more easily as an abuse of the parental role. It's not so noticeable when a mother does it, because she is intimate with a child anyway.'

With older boys abused by women who are not their mothers, society's attitudes, as mirrored in the tabloid papers, are another reason why the abuse isn't taken seriously. Whereas an adult man who had sex with a twelve-year-old girl would probably be described as a 'beast' or a 'monster', the experiences of a twelve-year-old boy with an older woman would be more likely to be described as 'love lessons' or 'sex games'.

In the few cases that reach the courts, the sentences meted out are comparatively lenient. One 36-year-old woman found guilty of gross indecency against two twelve-year-old boys, having first given them whisky and cider, was put on probation for three years. A woman of twenty-one pleaded guilty to indecent assault on a fourteen-year-old boy – they had intercourse seven times – and was put on probation for two years. In the spring of 1988, a case hit the headlines in which a 37-year-old woman, the mother of five children, ran away with a friend's eleven-year-old son with whom she had become obsessed. Where the abuser is the child's mother, the courts take a sterner view. A 28-year-old woman who sexually abused her four-year-old daughter every night, and who told the police she could see nothing wrong in what she had done, was sentenced to two years in prison.

Certainly more cases of serious sexual abuse by women have been brought before the courts in the last year or two. There have been several at the Old Bailey, perhaps most notoriously one in which the father as well as the mother was accused of sexually abusing their four children. The prosecution collapsed when one of the children broke down in the witness box. The mother was later sentenced for cruelty and neglect of her eight-year-old daughter.

And other sources are beginning to reveal that the number of women abusers, although still small compared with men, is actually quite significant. Studies in the USA have found that up to 4 per cent of girls are abused by women and up to 20 per cent of boys. Of the sexually abused boys who telephoned ChildLine in its first year, 38 per cent (some 400 children) had been abused by women: 18 per cent by their natural mothers, 8 per cent by sisters and 6 per cent by stepmothers. There were virtually no calls from girls who had been abused by women.

Kate Adams, an Incest Crisis Line counsellor in Essex, finds that the second most common category of calls she deals with, after father–daughter incest, are mother–son incest. Dr Estela Welldon, on the other hand, finds that the women who contact her are more likely to be concerned about incestuous relationships with their daughters than with their sons. 'Mother–son incest cases tend to come out only much later, and then usually via the son.'

American psychiatrists Summit and Kryso, among others, believe that mother–son incest is much more likely when the father has left, or died, and both are seeking comfort for his loss. They go on to make the point that even if incest does not take place, and the mother denies even the erotic potential of the situation, 'the boy can remain exclusively attached to her and have difficulties with sexual object choice in adulthood'.

Ruth (see p. 91) might well think they were talking about her husband, who abused their three children. 'His father was packed off abroad after his business failed when my husband was twelve, and from that moment his mother treated him as the man in her life. He told me she used to get him to brush her hair for hours, and though I don't think the relationship was sexually incestuous, emotionally and psychologically it most certainly was. She remained the dominant force in his life even when we married – everything was referred to her and was done as she liked it. He never committed himself to the marriage relationship with me and, as it turned out, he obviously never knew what a proper, adult, sexual relationship ought to be like.'

The most common way in which women abuse both boys and girls is by masturbation. '"Helping them to sleep" is a common pretext,' says Dr Welldon, 'or "it's easier than using a dummy". They move on to anal exploration sometimes, under the guise of putting in suppositories, for example, and oral sex. But it's not common for women to get children to masturbate them – that's so much more to do with men. With women, it's a compulsion to do to children, not to be done to.'

The fact that women abuse both sons and daughters is an indication to Richard Johnson that their motives in many cases are the same as those of male abusers. 'It's the abuse of a child, not the abuse of a sex, and you get women who are on power trips in just the same way as men are.'

With daughters, Estela Welldon believes, it might also have something to do with gender problems. 'A woman who is unsure of her sexuality might get pregnant as a way of resolving the problem. When the child is born, if it's a daughter, she may see something of herself in the child, and later on there may be some reawakening of homosexual feelings in her.'

When you start to explore the factors that make a man – or indeed a woman – abuse children sexually, you very quickly realize that there is no simple answer. You are dealing with beliefs and patterns of behaviour that have been established for forty or fifty *years* in some cases, and it is naive to expect that being caught and sent to prison, unpleasant though that undoubtedly is, will be enough to bring about a change. Certainly, it takes the abusers off the streets for a while, and where the abuse is within the family the social services may be able to ensure that the abuser never lives with his children again, at least until they are eighteen. What may happen then is that he moves on, finds a single-parent family, or has more children of his own and starts all over again. Or if he is reunited with his now grown-up family, who are no longer thought to be in danger, he may wait until the grandchildren begin to arrive and then abuse them.

Prison alone is not the answer, but although good work is being done in some places for the fortunate few, as we shall see in Chapter 6, that is all the majority of abusers get.

4 *Mothers*

One of the common myths about child sexual abuse, especially within the family, is that the mother always knows. How can she possibly live under the same roof as her children and her partner, the argument goes, and not know that something is going on? Even if the abuser isn't her partner but a stranger, and the abuse isn't just a one-off incident but goes on for some time, how can she fail to realize that something dreadful is happening to her child?

In Richard Johnson's experience, around 70 per cent of the mothers with whom he has come into contact genuinely hadn't the slightest idea what was going on. 'A large percentage of those would have known if they had opened their eyes, or perhaps, to be fairer, if they had known what to look for. The other 30 per cent certainly knew, and a good percentage of those were actively involved.'

Barbara puts herself in the category of those who would have realized if they had known what to look for. Her four-year-old daughter Louise was sexually abused frequently over an eight-month period, and maybe longer, by the father of her friend Amy. 'He made her masturbate him, give him oral sex, he penetrated her anally with the handle of a screwdriver and a knife, and often his wife would be taking photographs. But it's taken almost two years for Louise to tell me all this.'

Amy and her parents live just round the corner from Barbara, her husband and four daughters, and Louise, the youngest, often went out with them. It never occurred to Barbara – nor would it to any mother – that her daughter was at the slightest risk. 'Looking back now, there were signs while it was happening, but I just didn't have a clue then what they meant. She was always talking about willies, something my other three girls had never done. I even mentioned it to the health visitor and she said, "You often find this in a household where there are no boys – the girls are fascinated by boys' things." So I thought there was no reason to worry. She suffered from terrible cystitis and we were backwards and forwards to the doctor. In the end he just gave me a supply of medicine and cream and told me to use it whenever she got another attack. She became very disobedient and destructive, and for a while reverted to being a baby, wanting a bottle and for me to put her in nappies. When I didn't, she'd wet herself.

'It all came out because I was getting her undressed for the bath one day after she'd been to the park with Amy's family, and I found her knickers were on inside out. I asked her why and she said she'd been to the toilet. I said, "But you don't take your knickers off to go to the toilet," and then she said, "Paul did it." I asked why, and she answered, "Paul says I'm not allowed to tell you." That set the alarm bells ringing.

'I found out what I could and calmly got Louise ready for bed. My husband was out, so I got the fish-gutting knife out of the drawer, told my oldest daughter to keep an eye on the others and set out, fully intending to kill Paul. It was pouring with rain and, as I opened the door, my neighbour was on his step. He said, "Where on earth are you going in this?" I couldn't say, "Round the corner to kill the filthy bastard who's abused my daughter", so I said, "To my mum's." He said, "Hop in the van. I'll take you." If it hadn't been for that, I'd be inside now and that wouldn't have done my family a scrap of good.'

Even when mothers clearly don't know what has been going on, they blame themselves for not knowing and other people blame them too. Barbara's daughters blamed her for what happened to Louise and for not carrying out her original plan to kill the abuser. When Meg discovered her son Christopher had been abused by the parish priest, her husband blamed her for encouraging the relationship. 'He'd been every bit as pleased as I was that the man showed an interest in Chris, but I suppose he found the whole thing so unbearably painful that he had to blame someone.'

Some of the experts take the same line. As Elizabeth Ward points out in her book, *Father–Daughter Rape* (The Women's Press, 1984), in many studies there is a clear theme of 'mother-blaming' – sometimes unconscious, sometimes not. In one textbook, the authors maintain that if a woman denies her husband his 'conjugal rights, [he] may turn to the nearest available source of gratification – a dependent child'. Another states that if the mother withdraws from the family, her role may be taken over by a daughter, and the combination of the mother's absence and the role reversal may encourage 'the emergence of a dangerous relationship'.

The idea of the mother's behaviour as the *cause* of abuse in the family, which this line of argument suggests, ignores the four preconditions for sexual abuse, outlined by David Finkelhor and widely accepted by many professionals working in the field. Briefly, they are: first, that a potential abuser must have some motivation for abusing a child sexually (that his main sexual arousal is to children, for example); second, that he is able to overcome his own internal inhibitions (his morals, his concern for the child, and so on); third, that he is able to overcome external obstacles to the abuse – in other words, to create, or take advantage of, the circumstances in which it can take place; and fourth, he has to overcome the child's resistance to the abuse – by threats, bribery and other means.

So even if a mother, for whatever reason, allows the circumstances to arise where sexual abuse can take place, it won't unless there is already on the scene a potential abuser who has overcome his own inhibitions and the child's resistance.

As Danya Glaser, a child psychiatrist with wide experience in the field, points out in her book, *Child Sexual Abuse*:

> ... locating the origin of sexual abuse in the behaviour of mothers who are not fulfilling their roles produces a reading of abuse as a product of specific breakdowns in the smooth functioning of families, rather than as an intrinsic element in family life itself. Two common assumptions are observable here. The first is that child sexual abuse does not occur in 'healthy' families; hence if there is abuse, there must be distortion present in the way the family operates ... The second assumption, generally left unstated but frequently obvious, is that it is the role of women to create stability in family life, to maintain the health of the family system. Hence if the system becomes disturbed and abusive, the woman must have abandoned her role.

Psychologist Gerrilyn Smith sees 'mother-blaming' as part of society's punitive attitude to women: 'Society has an expectation that women ought to be able to protect their children from sexual abuse

– something that the combined efforts of the courts, the police, the law, social services and the medical profession cannot do – and then blames mothers when they can't.'

If a mother doesn't know that her children are being abused, then there must be good reasons. One reason could well be that she simply isn't around a lot of the time. In Anne's case (see Chapter 2), for example, her mother had two jobs for most of her childhood – an office job in the day and office-cleaning or a pub job in the evening – because Anne's stepfather was unemployed and they needed the money. This of course meant that he was at home all the time, 'looking after' Anne, which gave him every possible opportunity to abuse her. But even as a small child, Anne understood that her mother had to work, and didn't blame her for those absences. About other absences, though, she is much less forgiving. 'When I was seven I was a bridesmaid. It was something I'd always wanted to be, and I was thrilled. For some reason my stepfather wasn't there during the day, and it was brilliant, probably the best day of my life till then. He showed up at the reception, though, and kept going on about how lovely I looked. Just before it was time to go home, my mum disappeared – I know now she was seeing someone else – so I had to go home with him. He undressed me, not like a little girl but like a grown woman, and the sex went on the whole night. My day was totally ruined, and I hated my mum that night. I really, really hated her.'

Studies in the USA reach conflicting conclusions about whether children of working mothers are more likely to be abused. But certainly other studies show clearly that children whose mothers suffered from serious illnesses, physical and mental, and were either in hospital for long periods or invalids at home, were at greater risk of being abused than other children. In one study, over half the incest victims interviewed recalled that their mothers were away from home during their childhood as the result of illness.

In a recently published study carried out by Dr Bentovim and his colleagues at Great Ormond Street, of the 274 families referred to their sexual abuse unit between 1981 and 1986, 14 per cent of non-abusing parents (98 per cent of abusers in their study were men) had suffered either long-term or recent illness, and another 14 per cent had psychiatric problems.

In most cases illness is unavoidable, but in others, like Ruth's, it is a more complicated story. She had been married for seventeen years and had three children, two boys and a girl. 'The marriage was in trouble and I was very unhappy. My husband was totally dominated by his mother and didn't seem able to be loving or caring towards me or the children. Sexually he was insatiable – he wanted it two or three times a night four or five nights a week, but since there was never any affection or tenderness I found it very difficult to cope with, and distressing.

'As for the children, he didn't seem to know how to care for them when they were no longer babies, and was physically very rough with them. Most of the "games" he played with them ended in tears because he had hurt them.

'Five years earlier, we'd moved into a house. The basic building work had been done and then it was just left. My husband said we couldn't afford to pay anyone to get it straight and refused to do it himself. I tried, but it was too much for me, and besides, I got fed up, battling on on my own. As a result I was too ashamed to invite anyone to the house, and over that period I became increasingly isolated and depressed.

'In 1979, I had two breakdowns. The first was relatively minor, and the second, I'm sure now, was largely manipulated by him. It was almost as though he'd sat down and worked out a plan to get me out of the house. He told me I hadn't done or said things that I knew I had, and conversely that I'd done things that I hadn't. He told me that I'd threatened him and a neighbour with a knife; at that time I was still on quite heavy doses of tranquillizers from the first breakdown, so I couldn't be totally sure that I hadn't. (Some years later, though, he admitted to me that he'd made it all up and that I had never threatened anyone.) He also told our GP about it. Unfortunately, the doctor believed him and I was put into the local psychiatric hospital on a 28-day Section.

'When it was time for me to come out, my husband refused to let me come home. I was so doped up with tranquillizers that I didn't know he had no right to do that, and didn't have the strength to fight him, so I just went along with what he'd arranged and stayed with various friends for about six months.

'I discovered much later that he started buggering our eldest son, who was then eleven, and fondling the others at just about the time he'd had me committed to hospital. Whether or not this was all part of the plan I don't know, but what he had done to me meant that if I ever did become suspicious and wanted to report it, it was very unlikely anyone would believe me. Indeed when I did finally go to my GP with a statement my eldest son had written (as it turned out, a heavily censored version of the truth about what he had suffered at his father's hands), that's precisely what happened. Not only did he not believe me, he refused to examine or even talk to the children.'

It sometimes happens that the mother may be physically present but emotionally 'absent', unable to form a close relationship with her children. In some cases she herself may have been abused in childhood and so finds it very difficult to cope with emotional intimacy. In others, she may be so demoralized, so weighed down with problems of her own – a violent partner, for example – that she can't cope with her children's difficulties.

A number of studies carried out in the USA since 1956 have all found that women who were abused as children reported more distant relationships with their mothers than those who were not. In some cases, that means the child is forced to turn elsewhere for affection. If there is no father figure around, or if he too is cold, then the child becomes easy prey for an abusive outsider. If the father is around, then the child may well rely on him for all the affection she needs.

Liz was the eldest of seven children. Her mother treated her like a skivvy, knocked her about if she was ever disobedient and never showed her any affection. 'My dad was a very kind, caring person who never hit me, and when I was young we were very close. Then, when I was eleven, he abused me. He was gentle with me and didn't hurt me, but later he must have felt so guilty that he shut himself off from me, and hardly ever spoke to me any more. After that I got no affection from anyone. It was like sitting in a family of strangers.'

Interestingly, another common factor was found to be that women who had been sexually abused as children rated their mothers more punitive about sexual matters, less open, and less likely to have been the source of sex education (one way in which children might have been able to protect themselves against abuse), than those who had not been.

Paula's mother told her nothing at all about sex, and the only response she received to her questions about menstruation at the age of nine was silence from her mother and, soon afterwards, a practical, 'hands on' sex education lesson from her father.

In trying to understand why mothers who are not absent, either physically or emotionally, frequently don't know what is going on, Richard Johnson believes the desire and ability of children to cover up shouldn't be underestimated. 'Kids who are sexually abused become the world's best actors. They can cover up anything. After dad went to prison, I was a street prostitute for six years, and no one at home had the slightest idea. Before that, we kids all conspired to keep what dad was doing to us a deep, dark secret from mum. She was out working, sometimes up to eighteen hours a day, so that helped, but we actively chose not to let her know what was going on.'

There is also the fact that some children are terrified into silence, as in Oude Pekala, where the children were told their mothers would be killed if they told anyone. Much the same threats were made to Barbara's daughter, Louise. 'I eventually found out that he'd told her that if she said anything about it to us, we would kill her. He also said that if she told and we didn't kill her, then he would kill us. She knows we wouldn't hurt her, but she believes the rest of his threats. He has subsequently driven his car up on to the verge straight at my eldest daughter, has got a friend of his to break into our house, and has threatened to burn us out. So it's not surprising that she does.'

Even though children may say nothing, there are often clues to be found in their behaviour, as there were in Louise's. But it is only very recently that child sexual abuse has been talked about openly, or possible symptoms described, and what with hindsight seems glaringly obvious may well not have been so at the time. 'I think my mum was really stupid in many ways,' said Sue. 'My stepfather bought me a see-through baby doll nightie and negligée when I was eleven – the sort of thing you'd buy for a girlfriend – and said, "Go and try it on, then. Let's see how it looks." Another time my mum came and told me that she'd found a hole drilled in the wall between their bedroom and the bathroom – the one place where I'd thought I could lock myself away from him. She never said what she thought it was for, never mentioned it to him; she just filled it up.'

In other instances, there have been what seemed perfectly rational explanations for strange behaviour which mothers accepted. As Anne points out, if you live with a man, sleep with him, love him, it just never enters your head that he could be abusing a child, so you simply aren't looking for signs.

Rose knew that her daughter, Tina, was unhappy whenever her stepfather came home from sea, and was happy when he went back again. 'But I thought it was just that she got used to having me all to herself and resented having to share me with him when he came home. Obviously, if he was only home one week in six, I'd make a big fuss of him while he was there. Later, when it came out that he had been abusing her, she said she had tried to tell me in her own way. I just didn't pick up the signals. If I'd asked her outright if there was anything wrong, I think she would have told me.'

Richard Johnson's experience was similar. 'Mum knew we hated dad, but then he abused us physically very badly as well, so did she really need to look for any other reason for us to hate him?'

Even with physical symptoms, there are often plausible alternative explanations. 'If a small girl has a vaginal discharge,' said Gerrilyn Smith, 'her mother may well think, "It's because she's wearing nylon pants", or "It's the detergent I'm using." Most women would never think that their partner could possibly sexually abuse their child. The idea is still prevalent that it's strangers who abuse children — not the man the mother shares her bed with. That's the problem, and when the truth does hit, the reaction is often shock and then denial.'

A few months after she returned home from hospital Ruth's younger son Tim came to her and asked if what daddy had been doing to him was all right. 'I asked what he meant and he said that when he got into bed with dad for a cuddle, dad had fondled his genitals and made Tim fondle his. I said it wasn't all right but that maybe dad, half asleep, had thought it was me in bed beside him. I told Tim he was absolutely right to tell me, that I would talk to dad, and that if anything like it ever happened again he was to tell me. I talked to my husband. He agreed that it had happened, made no excuses for himself, but said he was sorry and that it wouldn't happen again. I asked if he'd interfered with the other two and he denied it.

'I didn't know what to do. I felt I couldn't go to my GP because of my history of mental breakdown, and anyway I wasn't convinced that it was more than a one-off incident. Tim never said anything else to me, so I left it.'

Sometimes mothers do suspect, but the ramifications of confirming those suspicions are so enormous that they choose not to follow them up. Richard Johnson believes that, on a subconscious level, his mother knew what was going on – certainly after one of his sisters, pregnant by his father, told her, if not before. 'Kate was so terrified of dad that at first she told mum it was a boy at work who'd got her pregnant. When she changed her mind and said it was dad, mum didn't believe her.

'As a child I resented mum for not protecting me, but later on in life I began to understand why she didn't do anything initially. She was like a lot of the mums I work with now. Her thinking was probably "(a) I don't understand the problem, therefore it doesn't exist; (b) if I confront this man with my suspicions and I lose him, how the hell am I going to support thirteen kids? and (c) I love this man passionately, even though he beats me as well as abusing my kids, and if I lose him my life will be over." For some reason, when I told her what had been going on when I was ten, she believed me, and immediately called the police.

'When he went to prison, mum loved him still, but she tried very hard to make up for what had happened to us, though by then it was too late. We were out of control. Later on, towards the end of her life, she tried hard not to allow us to take away from her the guilt that she felt. She would never let us make life a bit easier for her.'

When mothers do discover what has been going on within the family, their reaction is often stunned disbelief. It's not that they think the child is lying, but that the whole idea is so inconceivable they think there must be some mistake.

When Sheila (see p. 74) was telephoned by her daughter Angela's headmaster and asked to go up to the school urgently, she thought there had been more problems with other children teasing and bullying her. 'He told me it looked as though my husband, Angela's stepfather, had had sexual relations with her. I was flabbergasted that he even gave credence to such a story – I was sure it was something the other children had made up – and I said, "You'll see there's nothing wrong at home." He hadn't spoken to Angela himself, the deputy head had, and when I talked to her it was clear that there was more to it. They said to me, "Either it's true and your husband has a serious problem, or it's not, it's fantasy, in which case Angela has." From the moment I learnt that Angela herself had told them, I knew it was true. She would never lie, I knew that.'

The circumstances in which the abuse is discovered must have an effect on the intensity of a mother's reaction. Being told about it is bad enough. Actually walking in on it is something else. Rose had had a row with her husband in the club where they'd spent the evening, and he'd gone home early. When she followed an hour or so later, she found her key wouldn't turn in the lock. She knocked but there was no answer. Eventually, with the help of two lads leaving a local party, she climbed through a first-floor window.

'My sister's kids were staying over that night and my nephew was sitting on the stairs. I asked him what he was doing there, but he didn't answer. I went into my daughter's room. Her bed was empty. I ran into my son's room. She wasn't there, or in the living-room. I looked at my own bedroom door – it seemed about twelve feet high, I remember – and thought, "Oh no. It's not possible." I pushed the door open, and there was my daughter, sitting up in our bed, crying her eyes out, one side of her face all swollen. I learnt later that my husband had punched her because she'd refused to kiss him.

'I know my husband was there, but I didn't really see him. In fact it's all pretty much of a blur. I didn't even know what had happened exactly, but I just knew I had to get her out of there. I picked her up, ran to the living-room, wedged a chair under the door handle and rang the police. People often said to me afterwards, "If that had been me, I'd have gone to the kitchen, picked up the breadknife, run back into that bedroom and stuck it in him." But I don't think they would. You're operating on instinct, and your instinct tells you that your child's in danger and you just want to get her away as fast as possible. It's only much later that you think about the knife; by that time he was at the police station, and my daughter and I were on the way to the nearest police surgeon twenty miles distant for her to be examined.'

As soon as the police had taken her husband away, Rose felt compelled to have a bath. 'All the kids came into the bathroom with me, and we were talking quite normally. But I just felt so dirty, as though I would never be clean again. I understand how rape victims feel. I felt as though I'd been raped by a stranger myself. It's very, very hard when you discover that the man you once loved, the man you're married to, has done that to your child and the next day, or even the very same day, had sex with you.'

It wasn't until about ten days later that Rose's memories of her own experiences at her father's hands came flooding back. 'I'd made sure that I'd buried it all very deep inside because I didn't want to remember, but all the feelings came flooding back because I knew exactly how my daughter felt. I felt so guilty because it had happened to me, and yet I still hadn't been able to pick up the clues. Later on, I realized that it was foolish to blame myself like that. I'd never blamed my mother because my father had abused me. I know from personal experience that it can happen without anyone knowing or picking up any clues.'

From the time her daughters reached the age she was when her father had abused her, Paula was constantly on her guard when he was around them, afraid to leave them alone in the same room with him. 'My mother used to insist the girls went to stay with them, and I just found it impossible to refuse. But it was a nightmare the whole time they were away. I couldn't sleep, and when they came home I was constantly looking for signs and trying to encourage them to tell me if anything had happened. Soon after the last visit, we watched the second BBC "Childwatch" programme together and talked about it. I thought that if anything would trigger a disclosure that would, and when neither of them said anything, I did feel relieved.

'About a month later, a girl in my younger daughter's class broke down at school and revealed that she had been abused. My daughter also broke down and said it had happened to her. It was a Friday afternoon and the teacher told her she had to tell me that weekend or else she, the teacher, would do so on Monday.

'She came crying to me as though she was going to burst, and uttered the words I'll remember all my life: "Grandad's touched me." My immediate response was, "I believe you", but then I crumpled, crying, apologizing for allowing it to happen. I ran downstairs to the phone, rang him, and screamed, "This time you're not going to get away with it!" He said the same words he'd said to me as a child: "Get her examined. She's still a virgin." I told him I was going to contact the police and slammed the phone down. I did, and they and the social services became involved, but that was a whole other nightmare.

'At first I wanted him punished, but then I just wanted someone in authority to warn him and stop him doing it to any other children. My sisters, who have daughters, chose to believe him, not me, and so they still see him. I believe those children are at risk.

'As for me, the experience nearly shattered my life for the second time. I was in a hell of a state, and really had nowhere to go for help. If it hadn't been for the love and support of my second husband, I think I would have fallen apart.'

Although Meg's son Christopher wasn't abused by a relative, the effect on her relationship with him, and on the whole family, has been devastating. 'It was months before I felt able to cuddle him again. He couldn't bear to be touched, and I just felt so disgusted not with him, but at the idea of what had happened . . . we couldn't cope with each other. It's a bit better now, but it's still very difficult. Sometimes he'll say to me, "I wish this nightmare was over. How long is it going to take me to forget?" and I can't answer him.

'His three older sisters wouldn't go near him for months, my husband took to drinking heavily, and Chris's temper is still terrible. I would never have dreamt that something like that could cause so much damage. I don't think the family will ever be the same again. I actually long to see the priest who did it dead, and I never thought I would feel like that about anyone.' Perhaps the only thing Meg might have cause to be grateful for is that the abuser wasn't a member of the family, so there was no question of divided loyalties.

Nor is there any question for many women who are related to the abuser of their child. Paula had not one second's doubt about whose side she was on when her daughter disclosed that her grandfather had abused her, or that her relationship with her father was at an end. There was no question in Rose's mind either. Her marriage was over from the moment she walked into her bedroom and found her husband in bed with her daughter.

For other women, even though they believe their child, the choice is far less straightforward. Sheila, for instance, has never seriously considered divorcing Bill, partly because she doesn't want to and partly because her daughter Angela begged her not to right from the start. 'She was terrified of the family being split up – that's why she had never said anything about the abuse to me. She had been really scared by my inability to cope alone on our farm after her real dad had died and she dreaded me being in that position again.

'As for my feelings about Bill, right at the beginning he was so racked by remorse and so suicidal that I just couldn't attack him. I was genuinely terrified that he might commit suicide. And besides, he admitted from the start that it was entirely his responsibility and that Angela had always said no.

'The best part of the next year was spent trying to get first Angela and then Bill home again. Richard Johnson told us that the best chance we had of getting Angela home was if Bill moved out, so he went to live with my parents in Kent for eight months till it was all sorted out.

'Now I find I am very spiteful to him sometimes. He says he doesn't think I can ever forgive him. But his judgement on himself is so harsh that I do feel quite sorry for him. He suffers from terrible back and neck pain but his osteopath says there is nothing mechanically wrong with him – he is so full of guilt, so tense and stressed, that he is causing himself great pain.

'As for me, I did feel that what had happened was proof positive that I was a hopeless wife and a hopeless mother too. He's quite a bit younger than me, and I did also wonder whether I was past my best and he found Angela more attractive than me. But now I don't think that had anything to do with it.'

Richard Johnson finds that mothers who discover their daughters have been abused by their own sexual partners are quite often jealous, even if they don't acknowledge it consciously. 'I'm sure that was a factor in my mum refusing to believe my sister Kate when she first told her what was going on. You have to remember that mum loved dad very deeply; you had the classic situation where Kate had become a very sexual child as the result of the abuse and, though I don't suppose mum was aware of it, as far as she was concerned Kate was the "other woman" getting attention from dad.'

Other mothers respond to the discovery of sexual abuse in the family by refusing to believe the child, or by blaming her for the fact that it happened, or, if they do accept that it's going on, doing nothing about it. As Judith Lewis Herman put it in her study of women who had been sexually abused by their fathers, *Father–Daughter Incest* (Harvard University Press, 1981):

> Most of the mothers, even when made aware of the situation, were unwilling or unable to defend their daughters. They were too frightened or too dependent on their husbands to risk a confrontation . . . They made it clear to their daughters that their fathers came first and that if necessary the daughters would have to be sacrificed.

That's exactly what happened in Sue's case. Her mother chose to stay with her stepfather and half-brother Peter, while Sue from the age of thirteen was farmed out to a series of relatives. 'Mum did say to me once that she was only staying put for Peter's sake, and that when he was old enough she'd leave and we'd be a family again. I believed her. But Peter's nineteen now and she's still there.'

In other cases, mothers who find themselves unable to cope with the marital and sexual problems that have arisen allow their daughters to take over their role in the family – if you like, to shield them from the demands of their husbands rather than face the consequences of the break-up of the marriage. In the study carried out by Dr Bentovim and his colleagues at Great Ormond Street, it was found that over 60 per cent of the mothers involved reported having marital problems, over 30 per cent sexual problems, and 34 per cent were beaten by their partners.

Paula feels very strongly now that her mother used her as a shield against her father. 'For as long as I can remember he treated her with total contempt. He even used to fondle her sexually in front of us when we were small children, and he used to give her the most terrible beatings. Afterwards she would say she was going to divorce him, but the next day, it would be as though it had never happened.

'He started sexually abusing me after I'd asked her what periods were. He wasn't around at the time, so presumably she must have told him. After it started, she made it worse. She'd make me go up and wash his back in the bath, and she would never allow me to lock the bathroom door when I was in there.

'After the sexual abuse stopped, he became very violent to me. And when the violence came, my mother would blame me for making him angry. For a long time I thought she didn't know what he'd been doing. But looking back, I think she did know; she definitely used me as a shield.'

Not surprisingly, Paula feels as bitter about her mother as she does about her father. As a child she did feel sorry for her, but now, as the full impact of the damage done to her hits home and she recognizes her mother's part in it, she can't afford to be so compassionate.

Anne Bannister, as a more detached professional, can afford to be more forgiving. 'We don't blame mothers here *ever* – except if they are actively involved in the abuse of their own children.' (See Chapter 3.) 'That's not to say they are irrelevant – they are tremendously important in the dynamic, but very often they are victims too.

'If a mother went along with the abuse out of fear, then you have to ask what it was in her own scenario that made it impossible for her to be strong, to speak up and make a big fuss. And we know that 60 to 70 per cent of mothers of abused children were themselves abused. So we may well have to work on the question of why she married an abuser. Of course, she may not have known consciously that he was an abuser, but why do we choose our partners?' Psychologist Maria Mars takes the same view. 'You often find the mother is in an abusing relationship with the husband. She has been infantilized by him, treated as a child, so her capacity to protect her own child is greatly diminished. And that, maybe, is on top of a history of abuse in her own childhood.'

Although, as we shall see in Chapter 6, some treatment programmes do include help for mothers, they tend to be the forgotten victims in child sexual abuse. At the same time that they are trying to help their child recover from a dreadful trauma, they are also often battling against overwhelming feelings of pain and guilt that they failed to protect that child, no matter how impossible that may have been, feelings of murderous rage against the abuser and, all too often, frustration that the police are unable to bring him to justice. If the abuser is their partner, then there are feelings of betrayal and rejection

102 The Last Taboo

too, of grief for the past and the future there now cannot be, never mind all the practical problems of coping single-handed from then on. There are the other children, often being difficult, and the child who was abused, frequently not passive and pitiable, but violent, angry, destructive, moody, reproachful, overtly sexual . . . And all too often there is no one to turn to apart from a GP with a prescription for Valium.

That is not to say that abused children shouldn't remain the focus of attention. Of course they should. But for their sakes too, a lot more mother-supporting, rather than mother-blaming, wouldn't come amiss.

5 Society's Response

The events in Cleveland in 1987 showed most graphically many of the problems present in the current official response to child sexual abuse. For a start, concerned professionals – doctors, police surgeons, police officers, nurses, social workers – who should have been working together for the benefit of the children were either not speaking, or were at each other's throats. Then there were the terrible problems that can arise for families when children are taken into care – not knowing where they are, not being allowed to see them, not knowing when, or if, they will be allowed to return home.

Cleveland highlighted too the dangers of acting too quickly, and also the very real dilemma facing professionals. Do they get it wrong by failing to act, or do they act and risk getting it wrong?

Child sexual abuse has always created problems for a multi-disciplinary approach. Although the different groups of professionals concerned share a common goal of serving the child's best interests, in theory at least, they all approach it from different angles. The police, for instance, are concerned with collecting evidence for prosecuting the abuser. That means the child has to be interviewed in a particular way – no leading questions, for example, which would render the child's statement inadmissible as evidence. A doctor or a social worker, on the other hand, may well feel such questions are perfectly valid in achieving their main aim – helping the child to disclose the abuse, partly so that they know what action to take for her protection and partly because disclosing is a vital first step in the child's recovery. The same is true of physical examination. A police surgeon's priority is to find forensic evidence, using techniques that perhaps a paediatrician with no experience of police work would not know. All too often the result has been that a suspected victim is examined many times, an experience some children find almost as distressing as the abuse itself. In certain areas there have been very positive initiatives. The Metropolitan Police and the London

Borough of Bexley, for example, developed a scheme in which police officers and social workers are trained together and interview children jointly. However, that is still the exception rather than the rule and a conflict of interests is still quite common.

But in Cleveland it seemed that it went beyond a mere conflict of interests. Professional jealousies, personal feuds and public slanging matches led to a complete breakdown in communication between some groups. Police refused to attend some case conferences, police surgeons claimed that paediatricians prevented them from examining children, nurses were angered by the disruption caused to sick children in their wards by the influx of suspected sexual abuse victims, some social workers were upset by the fact that children had to go through so many medical examinations ... Even more alarming to the public was the fact that well over 100 children were whisked away from their parents under Place of Safety orders, apparently on the say-so of one doctor who diagnosed sexual abuse using a new and controversial technique, the validity of which was fiercely disputed by many experienced doctors.

In fact a Place of Safety order, which allows for the immediate removal of a child thought to be in danger to a 'place of safety' for up to twenty-eight days, is granted by a magistrate on application by the police, the local authority's social services department, or the NSPCC. The magistrate has to be satisfied that the child in question is in immediate danger. The MP for Stockton South, Tim Devlin, some of whose constituents were involved in the Cleveland affair, has suggested that judges rather than magistrates should issue Place of Safety orders. Magistrates, he believes, do not feel competent to challenge the professionals, and therefore usually go along with social services' recommendations.

Before the Place of Safety orders expired, many of the children in Cleveland were made the subjects of interim care orders by the local authority and kept away from their parents for months. In the case of one couple whose story was told in the *Mail on Sunday* in February 1988, it was nineteen months before their two daughters aged five and three were allowed to return home after a ruling by a judge. During that time the parents were denied proper access, were told by social services that there were plans for their daughters to be provided with 'a permanent alternative family with the intention that adoption will be the outcome', and it was made clear that, if they opposed that plan, any children they might have in the future were at risk of being removed at birth. The mother, who became pregnant during this time, had an abortion as a consequence.

It must be said that situations like this can arise in *any* child care proceedings, not just those involving child sexual abuse. While many parents in Cleveland do feel extremely bitter about Dr Higgs, it is totally unfair to lay the blame for what followed from her diagnoses – right or wrong – at her door.

THE CARING PROFESSIONS

One problem with child care proceedings lies in the fact that these are civil proceedings which require a different quality of proof from criminal proceedings. In the latter, the accused's guilt has to be proved 'beyond all reasonable doubt'. In the former, all that has to be proved is 'the balance of probability' ('it's more likely than not that he did it') so the evidence produced does not have to be quite so strong. In a case of child sexual abuse, for example, the police may decide that there is not enough evidence to prosecute the child's father, but social workers and doctors may still be able to convince a magistrates' court that their suspicions are sufficiently well grounded to warrant removing the child from her parents and placing her in care. It is also possible for a situation to arise in which a father is found not guilty by the courts, but social services still refuse to return the child home.

The other major problem with child care proceedings in England and Wales is that the wheels of justice can grind exceeding slow. (In Scotland procedures are different and much speedier. See p. 115.) Where adults are concerned, the law's delay can be destructive enough, but with children it can be absolutely catastrophic. A year in the life of a three-year-old child is an eternity, certainly long enough for her to forget her natural parents and to make settling in with them again extremely difficult. There have been instances where a case has taken such a long time to get to court that, although the judge has vindicated the parents and castigated social services for their action in removing the children, he has decided that the children have been with foster parents for so long that it would not be in their best interests to return them home.The same delays occur in the criminal justice system, too, though a recent Home Office directive has instructed the Crown Prosecution Service to speed up the process in cases of child sexual abuse.

The dilemma facing doctors and social workers was painfully highlighted by the Cleveland controversy. If they do nothing when confronted by a suspicion of child sexual abuse, they are possibly leaving a child exposed to further abuse and all its dreadful long-term consequences. If they act and are found to have been wrong, the system's delay in rectifying their errors can have consequences almost as damaging for a child as sexual abuse. Even if they are right, then the way things are, the cure – removing the child from her family, which however awful is the only security she knows, compounding her sense of guilt and her view of herself as a powerless victim – can be as damaging as the disease.

There is no doubt that for children, too, the Cleveland controversy has already made an impact. 'ChildLine', the national helpline for children in trouble and danger, found in its first year that the overwhelming majority (95 per cent) of children calling to talk about abuse will only give their first name, not their full name and address, for fear of being removed from their families if they tell.

'They will say, "I want him to stop it, but I don't want you to take him away,"' said ChildLine's director Valerie Howarth, 'or, "They won't take me into care, will they?"

'Cleveland focused on the way that, all too often, we deal with child abuse, which is by *not* listening to the children. We put in some very simple evidence to the Cleveland inquiry which was that, in our experience, what most children are saying is that they don't like their families being broken up, and they don't see why they should be the ones removed from home.'

In Cleveland, doctors and social workers were actively looking for child abuse. In most other parts of the country it comes to light either because a child tells an adult – a parent or someone in authority – or because a parent, a teacher, a health visitor or a doctor comes across something suspicious that prompts further investigation – physical symptoms or the sort of behaviour described in Chapter 7, or a combination of the two. Sometimes a child who plucks up the courage to tell isn't believed. Some mothers still find it impossible to accept that the man they live with could do such a thing; others find the consequences of accepting it too frightening to contemplate.

The authorities don't always believe a child, either. Richard Johnson had a call from one girl who, after watching Esther Rantzen's 'Childwatch' programme on BBC TV, plucked up the courage to walk into her local police station and tell the desk sergeant what her father had been doing. 'He looked her full in the face and said, "Do you realize what this will do to your dad's reputation?", telling her, in so many words, to go away.'

Jane, a thin, nervous girl of eighteen, is extremely bitter about the lack of help she has received since social services first intervened in her family when she was ten and a suspected victim of physical abuse. 'My dad raped me the night before my tenth birthday, and was still beating me up, which is what they picked up on at school. Me and my sister were put into care, my dad was tried but found not guilty, so we were sent back home again. After that, the social worker would visit but she would never even try to get us on our own. She'd always ask us how things were in front of him. Of course we'd say we were getting on all right and yes, he was letting us go out. He'd stand there with this big grin on his face, as if to say, "If you're stupid enough to say all that, fine!" After she'd gone, he'd often thump us for not telling the truth! If social services had done their job, I wouldn't have gone through eight years of hell.'

To be fair, until very recently few professionals – social workers or doctors – had any training at all on the subject of child sexual abuse, and for those who did it was rarely for more than a couple of hours. It is also true to say that it is a topic about which many professionals, like many members of the public, are still, personally, very uncomfortable.

'After the disclosures in my family, and the medical examination,' said Richard Johnson, 'a social worker popped her head round the door and said, "You know where I am if you need me!" Then she ran so fast we couldn't see her backside for dust. Later we discovered she was the expert on child sexual abuse because she hadn't been able to run as fast as everyone else when the first case came in!'

According to Professor Sydney Brandon of Leicester University, who is also Chairman of the new Training and Advisory Group on the Sexual Abuse of Children, the situation today isn't a great deal better. 'With some outstanding exceptions, we must acknowledge that our professions and our services are on the whole failing to cope with the challenge of sexual abuse.'

Adults who report sexual abuse of their children aren't always believed, either. One woman, worried about her children, went to five different agencies to express her concern. She was reassured by every one of them that there was nothing to worry about, and when it finally emerged that the children had been sexually abused, they were taken into care on the grounds that she had failed to protect them.

When Ruth, whose story was told in Chapter 4 (see p. 91), discovered that her husband had sexually abused their three children, she took her eldest son's statement about it to her GP. 'He read it, then said, "Well, this is all very difficult, isn't it? You've been in a mental hospital under a compulsory order, you've been on powerful drugs, and you've complained about the marriage for some time . . .", and shrugged. He was obviously implying that I was crackers. It ended in a slanging match because he refused even to see any of the children, let alone examine them.'

When Paula discovered that her father, who had abused her as a child, had also abused her own eleven-year-old daughter, she telephoned him, screamed, 'This time you're not going to get away with it!' and then rang the police.

'The police and social workers came round and took a statement from my daughter, and then one from me about my experiences as a child. That was very traumatic. Things surfaced that I'd blocked for well over twenty years; I could even smell my father as I recounted everything. They left, and I felt stripped of everything: dignity, pride, self-worth. No one supported us or helped us as a family.

'Two months later, as nothing had happened, I rang the local police. The young detective constable I spoke to said, "Well, we thought over Christmas you and your father might have patched things up. Do you still want us to go ahead?" I said, "Of course. He must be made to see that it's wrong."

'They did send someone to see him, then rang me back and said, "Your father wasn't at all happy about us going to see him, you know" – as though it was somehow my fault. Another few weeks passed, and then they decided not to prosecute because they said too much time had gone by between the "alleged" offence and my daughter's statement. They also said my daughter wouldn't be a good witness in court and, as my father was denying it, he would win. As far as the authorities were concerned, that was that.'

Disclosure

Of course very young children don't actually tell people they are being sexually abused, or even that someone is doing rude things to them, because such concepts mean nothing. But, to professionals trained to listen, even children as young as three or four can reveal what is going on. They say things like, 'My daddy makes holes in my knickers', and 'A snake comes in the night and bites my bottom.'

Psychologists Gerrilyn Smith, Maria Mars and Anne Peake run a consultation service for all professionals working with children in one London borough, so that anyone who is concerned about a particular child can come in and share those concerns.

'Over a nine-month period, in discussions about some seventy children, it was clear to us that forty-three of them had already disclosed sexual abuse, though the worker hadn't necessarily picked it up.

'What that means is that we then have to set up an artificial disclosure interview in order to get the child to say it all again in a way that is legally acceptable. It's as though we're saying to the child, "OK, you said it already but you didn't say it right."'

In most cases, according to Gerrilyn Smith, children are left at home pending investigation. 'Cleveland was unusual. It's a myth that social workers rush in and remove children at the merest suspicion. Most of them don't, and by not doing so, they hang on to a lot of anxiety about those children.'

There is always the danger, though, that once parents have been alerted to the fact that doctors or social workers suspect their child is being abused they may put a lot of pressure on the child to withdraw any disclosure she may have made, or block any attempts to persuade her to do so. Any professional in the field will tell you there are far more false withdrawals of allegations than there are false allegations.

However, Gerrilyn Smith points to the very real dangers inherent in acting too quickly. It's not just that innocent families can be caused terrible suffering; if the authorities act before they have enough evidence in families where children are being sexually abused, then the subsequent investigation clears the abuser and the children are returned home to face further abuse. 'A failed investigation is even more damaging than no investigation, because the abuser taunts the child: "See, I told you! No one can do anything to protect you."'

Richard Johnson agrees. 'I worked with one family involved in the recent controversy where I know for a fact that the father had been abusing his kids. The court has now returned those kids to their father.'

Anne Bannister, on the other hand, is very concerned that, in the wake of Cleveland, professionals will err on the side of caution. 'People working with child sexual abuse are saying, "Oh, we must be very careful. We mustn't just whip children away." I agree with that totally – you must assess every case very carefully. But if a child tells me that her father is sexually abusing her, and I say, "I believe you and that's terrible! But just go home to your dad now and we'll sort it all out," the message I'm giving her is either "I don't really believe you", or "I do believe you but it's not terribly important – you won't die of it!" So to an extent you are condoning the abuse, adding to the child's anguish and, again, confirming the abuser's message that no one will believe her, no one will do anything to stop it because really it's all right for this to happen.'

Suspicions of Abuse

If a child has not made any disclosure, but a professional – a teacher, social worker, GP or health visitor – suspects that she is being sexually abused, he or she is morally and ethically (though not legally) bound to report it to the person appointed by the local authority to coordinate child abuse cases in their area. Usually a case conference is then called where, ideally, all the professionals concerned, including the police, share their knowledge about the child in question.

What indicates child sexual abuse is rarely a single symptom (though obviously pregnancy in an eleven-year-old, or gonorrhoea in any child's vagina, anus or throat, is pretty damned conclusive), but a combination of symptoms which in isolation may look fairly harmless.

In the Great Ormond Street sexual abuse team's recent book, *Child Sexual Abuse within the Family* (John Wright, 1988), Dr Eileen Vizard and her former colleague Marianne Tranter describe one such conference about a four-year-old girl whose behaviour made her teacher suspicious that she could have been sexually abused.

Having explained the need for information-sharing to the group, the chairperson gathered various items of information about the family background, and asked the GP if there was anything relevant in the notes. The GP replied angrily, 'Well, not unless you count some recurrent vulvovaginitis [redness and irritation of the genital area often caused by poor hygiene but also sometimes by sexual abuse] a few weeks ago, but on that basis, half the four-year-olds in my practice would be abused!'

If, as the result of such a conference, it seems likely that the child has been sexually abused, the next step is a medical examination and an interview, ideally (in both cases) conducted by people specially trained in dealing with sexually abused children.

But, as we know, the various professional groups involved have different needs. In many places, not just in Cleveland, the results of this are poor personal relationships and a lack of communication between the professionals and, for the child, an endless round of interviews. To try and solve this problem, the London Borough of Bexley and the Metropolitan Police pioneered a scheme in 1985 in which social workers and police officers are trained together in joint interviewing techniques and work in pairs with children who have suffered various kinds of abuse. The scheme has been so successful that the Metropolitan Police have adopted it as the basis for a new force-wide strategy, and it is hoped that it will be implemented in all the forty London boroughs in which they operate by the end of 1989.

Children cannot be medically examined without their parents' permission, and if parents refuse to give it, then the social services may apply for a Place of Safety order to remove the child from home. Although in many cases the local authority would then have the child medically examined, some lawyers would argue that they have no right to do so and that technically they could be guilty of assault. A Place of Safety order doesn't give them parental rights; it simply allows them to remove the child to a place of safety. To assume parental rights, they would then have to apply to a magistrates' court for an interim care order. Having obtained the order, they could give permission for the child to be examined.

This is still a grey area, as is the question of whether doctors who are examining a child for one reason have the right to look for symptoms of something else without asking the parents' permission. In Cleveland, some parents are now suing the doctors concerned for assault.

As doctors become increasingly aware of the nature of child sexual abuse, there is a great deal more sensitivity in examinations these days. Some doctors include an examination of the genital area simply as part of an overall medical, for instance, and appear to give it no more attention than, say, eyes or chest. Just as important is the growing awareness of the need to keep the number of medical examinations to the minimum, for the child's sake. Some children in Cleveland were alleged to have been examined over twenty times.

In the last few years, much attention has been paid to the development of the skills needed in interviewing children (or making assessments of children who are too young to interview) who are suspected of having been sexually abused, and helping them to disclose.

Anne Bannister of the N S P C C and Great Manchester Authorities Sexual Abuse Unit in Manchester has wide experience in this area. 'A disclosure interview, at least the way we do it here, is also the beginning of therapy for the child, so it's done in a therapeutic setting and in a therapeutic way. I usually work with the social worker involved, the residential worker if the child is in a children's home, or the foster parent, and they are either in the room with me or behind a one-way mirror. That's partly because it's important for them to see that I don't wave a magic wand or do anything extraordinary, and I hope they will carry on and do the long-term work with the child. I am firmly opposed to the idea that you have "special" child sexual abuse centres that do this incredibly special work that, it's thought, ordinary social workers or foster parents can't possibly do. Also, because secrecy is such a crucial element in sexual abuse, we make sure that there's no secrecy in this unit. They can see exactly what I'm doing.'

In Anne's room there are several different areas – a dolls' house (with white or black or Asian dolls as appropriate), puppets, drawing materials, and what she calls 'anger' toys, things a child can thump or bang. 'The children choose what they want to do and I help them, play with them. I don't just watch them play. I'll look out for a particular feeling or emotion and encourage it. If it's a feeling of anger, I encourage the child to bang the pegs or whatever. Then I'll say, "Who are we angry with?" Often a child will say "My little brother or sister" – that's a safe focus for their anger – so I'll say, "OK, let's thump the pegs for your little brother or sister." Then gradually, as the child comes to trust you a bit more, you can push a little and find out who they are really angry with. It's not pressuring the child. It's allowing the child to express feelings more easily.'

Anne also has great faith in the use of psychodrama, for adults and children, as a means of exploring in a safe environment the trauma they have suffered. 'What children usually do anyway is act out in metaphor. They think in symbols. A child might say, "The monster comes in the night to me", and it takes a lot of work before daddy and the monster can become one and the same.

'I work mostly with dolls and puppets first, before doing direct psychodrama, because the abuse is either still happening or is very recent and it's much easier for the child to work in the third person. Later on we can move on to direct psychodrama, though usually I will play the abused child because it's much too scary for the child to do so.'

The whole time, Anne is listening carefully to what the child is saying. 'They will test you out. They will say something "rude" to see if you're going to be shocked. If you are, and you punish them, they won't tell you any more. If you're not, they will go on. I always repeat what they've said. If a child says, "Then he got his willie out," I say, "Then he got his willie out." I've confirmed to the child that I've heard, that I can say the word, that they can say the word, and so then they tell me the next bit.

'I try very hard not to put pressure on a child, or ask any direct questions, because on the whole I don't think children respond well to pressure – it sends them backwards. But I can't put my hand on my heart and say that I never do, because occasionally you get a very tricky situation. A child has said something ambiguous, maybe, so that someone is extremely worried that they may be victims of sexual abuse. If you do nothing, then the child will go straight back home to the family.

'In that situation, if the child isn't giving anything away, towards the end of the interview I might ask some direct questions. I am aware too from my work with adult victims that they will often say, when asked why they never told anyone they were being abused, "Nobody ever asked me."'

Other doctors and social workers work in a similar way with young children, using play and drawings to help them communicate experiences that they can't put into words, or find too painful to speak about. Many use anatomically correct dolls – adult and child dolls with vaginas, anuses, penises and mouths – and simply observe how the child plays with them. Some people are critical of this method on the grounds that all children, abused or not, are curious about genitals, or that the dolls themselves may sexualize children. Research suggests they are wrong. One study done by Dr Danya Glaser of eighty non-sexually abused children between the ages of three and six, both boys and girls, found that only three of the children showed any persisting interest in the dolls' genitals; the vast majority, after a cursory glance at them, played with the dolls in a perfectly ordinary way – washing their faces, telling them off, taking them to school, and so on. Another small-scale study carried out in the USA with ten matched pairs of children – one who was known to have been sexually abused and one who hadn't – between the ages of three and eight, found that nine of the ten sexually abused children demonstrated sexual behaviour (including vaginal, oral and anal intercourse) between the dolls, while only two of the ten non-abused children did so. On further investigation it was discovered that those two children were actually in care, and though no one had previously suspected it, there was a chance that they too might have been abused. The team at Great Ormond Street also found that some abused children are afraid, or at least unwilling, to touch the doll representing their probable abuser. Other children react violently to it, like one three-year-old boy in their study who punched and stabbed the abuser doll with a crayon – an outlet of emotion that the team considered very therapeutic.

There is also a danger that anatomically correct dolls become thought of as the definitive method of getting children to disclose sexual abuse. Get a set of those and all your problems will be over! Skilfully used, they can be very valuable, but they are no substitute for a well-trained, sympathetic interviewer.

But in some cases, no matter how skilled the interviewer the child won't disclose everything in one session. It may take weeks, or even years, for the whole story to emerge. Even two years after Barbara first found out what had happened to her daughter, Louise, who is now six, is still giving her new information.

CIVIL PROCEEDINGS

Once medical evidence has been obtained and/or the child has disclosed enough information, a case conference is called to decide what to do next. In the past, although other professionals could make recommendations which were often accepted, the decision about whether to prosecute an abuser remained with the police. Since the introduction of the Crown Prosecution Service in England and Wales last year, the police no longer prosecute. Instead, they investigate and pass on their findings – including the views of the case conference – to the Service, who then make the decision.

In Scotland the system is different. Any worker concerned about the possible abuse of a child informs the reporter to the Children's Hearing, the system set up in 1971 to replace juvenile courts. The reporter then investigates the facts of the case and the child's background, and decides whether a Children's Hearing should be held to consider the need for some kind of compulsory care. If he decides it should be held, it must be arranged within seven days. If he decides against, he may refer the child and the family to the local authority for help. The job of the Hearing is not to establish questions of guilt or innocence but to decide on whether the child needs compulsory care or not. If the 'grounds for referral' are disputed – if the parents deny abuse, for example – then the case is referred to the sheriff court for 'proof'. If it is decided that the 'grounds for referral' are confirmed, the case returns to the Children's Hearing. If they are not, then the referral will be discharged. When parents disagree with the Hearing's findings, they have the right of appeal to the Sheriff court, and the appeal must be heard within three days.

In one recent case which made legal history in Scotland, local authority social workers wanted to remove from her parents a four-year-old girl they suspected of being sexually abused, but the parents denied abuse and opposed the moves to take the child into care. When the case was referred to the Glasgow sheriff court, the sheriff took all the court officials and lawyers involved to the city hospital and watched through a one-way mirror as the girl played with anatomically correct dolls. As a result of what they saw, the sheriff ordered her to be taken into care.

In England and Wales, social services have to consider the future of the child, regardless of any decision about a criminal prosecution. If they have sufficient grounds to convince a court that she has been or is being sexually abused within the family, their local authority can apply either for wardship proceedings or for a Place of Safety order. When a child becomes a ward of court, the court takes over the rights and duties of the parents and makes all the decisions about her welfare – whether or not she will be taken into care, for example, or left at home. It is a slower process than a Place of Safety order, and all parties concerned (parents, the local authority and the child) are represented.

A Place of Safety order, granted by a magistrate, means that the child is removed from her parents on the spot and can be kept in 'a place of safety' for up to twenty-eight days. (In practice it tends to be less – eight or fourteen days is more common.) The parents have no right of appeal against it.

In Gerrilyn Smith's experience, the choice of wardship or a Place of Safety order often depends, not on the severity of the offence, but on the social class of the offender. 'If it's a nice, white, middle-class man who's been abusing his children, they are much more likely to go for wardship and leave the children at home. That gives him time to marshal his defences, move out of the house, maybe get private treatment for himself or his children, and negotiate with the social services. If he is poor, working-class, and from an ethnic minority, then it's much more likely to be a Place of Safety order, followed by an Interim Care order, and the kids are removed at once. You don't negotiate with a social worker waving a Place of Safety order.'

Sheila's thirteen-year-old daughter Angela was taken away by local social workers after she had disclosed at school that her stepfather had been sexually abusing her (see p. 98).

'A lot of pressure was put on Angela by the school, by the social worker they'd called in and by the police to "confess". She was not treated kindly or offered support. She was not told what the likely outcome would be or that she didn't have to answer. Criminals are told they have the right to remain silent, but a child who had done nothing wrong wasn't given that option.

'They had been to court, without any knowledge of us as a family at all, to get a Place of Safety order, and they told me they were taking Angela to a children's home. She was in a terrible state, begging me not to let them take her. But there was nothing I could do. She was told at first that it was for one night only. Then she was told that she'd have to stay till the case conference, then till the case conference after that ... At one point she said to me, "I don't think I'll ever come out of here."

'They kept her away for three weeks, and she felt very unhappy and guilty that it was all her fault. She often said that she wished she'd never said anything, because she was so frightened about what would happen to her stepdad and to the rest of us. And she felt that in being whisked away she was being punished, so it had to be her fault.'

Feelings of anger among children in that situation are very common indeed. After all, they've done nothing wrong, and yet they're the ones who are being punished by being taken away from their family and friends, their toys, their schools, while the abuser is often still at home. For others like Angela, the fact that they are being punished simply confirms their guilt. Richard Johnson is not alone in believing that in these situations the abuser, not the child, should be removed from home as is done in some states in the U S A. 'If a number of children had disclosed that a local resident, not a relative of any of them, had been abusing them, social services wouldn't come in and remove those kids. The police would come in and remove the alleged offender. That's what I'd like to see happening when the abuse is within the family.' So would the NSPCC, according to its director, Dr Alan Gilmour, in the Society's 1987 Report.

Place of Safety?

An added problem is that 'place of safety', and indeed 'care', is often a misnomer. Sheila's daughter Angela, whom she describes as 'a very immature, sheltered thirteen-year-old', was mixing in the children's home with youngsters who drank and used drugs. 'There was only one member of staff on at night and the kids would go off to the local pub. When I left after a visit, there'd be gangs of motor-bike boys snogging with the girls from the home. They told Angela things like, "Oh, your mum'll lose interest after a few weeks and you won't see her again", which upset her terribly.'

What happened to Richard Johnson's thirteen-year-old niece Annie after she disclosed that she had been sexually abused by her father was a nightmare. 'She was taken into care by the local authority and put in an assessment centre where, within a short space of time, she was sniffing glue, shoplifting, and so on. Because she was "anti-social" she was sent to a secure establishment, with locks and warders and so forth, although she had committed no crime. Within weeks she was raped by a thirteen-year-old boy in the home and became pregnant. By the time the baby was born she was into heroin and cocaine, which were freely available in the home, and the baby had to be detoxified because it was born addicted. She then went into a series of half-way houses and disappeared. It's only quite recently that we've heard from her again. She's living in the USA (where she grew up) with her child, and is finally getting her life together.

'Her father, incidentally, stood up in court, readily admitted to sexually abusing her and her brother for over ten years in the USA, but denied ever doing it once they arrived back in this country; he walked away, a free man, on a technicality.'

Sadly, what happened to Annie isn't an isolated instance. The National Association of Young People in Care reports any number of cases where children have been sexually abused by staff or other residents of children's homes. Occasionally scandals surface, like that in Greenwich in 1987. And according to one social worker, who has seen it happening in both London and Newcastle, pimps are actually working children's homes, recruiting for child prostitution and pornography.

Many local authorities prefer to place children with foster parents if they can. But children who have been sexually abused can be very difficult to handle – they often know only one way of relating to adults and that is sexually, which can be extremely disturbing for an ordinary foster parent who has no experience of such behaviour and simply isn't prepared for it. They may find it very unpleasant to hear a child talk about her experiences, and their disgust may transmit itself to the child as confirmation of her own guilt and worthlessness. Or they may be anxious in case the child may talk to their own children, or even re-enact the abuse with them.

There is also the risk of re-abuse. A child who has already been sexualized by previous abuse is obviously at great risk from anyone who is sexually aroused by children. Bill, now in his late sixties, is a self-confessed paedophile who was on the books of several different fostering agencies for many years, fostered over two hundred children, and molested many of them (see pp. 61, 64). The point is that foster parents aren't very easy to find, Bill had no criminal record, his references were excellent, and, like many paedophiles, he was extremely good at covering his tracks.

Going Home

As to the child's long-term future, the key factor in any decision about returning a child home is the ability of the non-abusing parent – usually the mother – to protect the child from further abuse. For most doctors and social workers the essential point is that she admits the abuse has happened, believes the child and doesn't hold her in any way responsible for it. If she doesn't believe the child, or she believes the child is as much to blame for what happened as the abuser, then the risk of further abuse is usually considered too great to return the child home. That is a perfectly reasonable view to take where a child has been abused by someone in the family. But if the parents are innocent, it can create a nightmarish 'Catch 22' situation, as Russell Miller's account of one family caught up in the Cleveland affair showed only too vividly (*Sunday Times Magazine*, 29 May 1988). Unless the father accepts responsibility for the abuse and the mother accepts that it has happened, their children are very unlikely to be returned home. If they do admit it in an attempt to get their children home, the father risks criminal prosecution and the family may well be broken up anyway.

In some cases, too, a mother admitting the abuse has happened, believing the child and not blaming her, isn't, in a sense, considered enough. 'The social workers treated me as an abuser too,' said Sheila, 'and they were very spiteful in little ways. The children's home where Angela was staying was miles away from where we lived and involved a very complicated train journey, but they wouldn't even let Bill's parents drive me there and drop me off.

'The fact that I wouldn't divorce Bill and wanted to reunite the family annoyed them. They seemed to take the view that I must have known, and in that case the only way to prove my innocence was by starting divorce proceedings against my husband. They did say on several occasions that if I wanted Angela back I would have to do that.

'When I told them Bill had gone to stay with my parents 150 miles away from our home and asked if it would be all right for Angela to come back, they said, "But *you're* still there!" When I became very ill from all the stress, they said I was too neurotic to be a good parent.'

Rose, too, still bears the scars from her dealings with social workers in Scotland after she discovered her daughter had been abused by her husband. 'Luckily there was no danger of my daughter being taken into care, because my husband was in custody, but the social worker obviously thought I had colluded in the abuse. It came out in conversations with her that I had been abused myself as a child, but when I refused to go into all the details she said that she would tell the reporter to the Children's Hearing I was an un-cooperative parent. She also said that because I had been molested as a child and had done nothing about it, I had married my husband knowing he would molest my daughter!

'In a situation like that, you are destroyed inside anyway, you are totally devastated. And on top of it all, to be handled so in-sensitively by people in the "caring" professions just twists the knife. I felt suicidal for months, and I still do on black days. I think I survived because I had my family behind me.'

Gerrilyn Smith and her colleague Maria Mars believe it is very important for professionals not to lose sight of the fact that, on the whole, men abuse and women don't. 'We don't see the parents automatically as a colluding little lump, perpetrating the abuse. We try and work with the mother, supporting her and giving her the information and the strength she needs to protect her child. Often it's a tough choice for a woman to make. One consequence may be poverty, and if she has been in an abusive relationship with a man her self-esteem may well be so low that the thought of coping alone is terrifying.

'But society gives mothers very mixed messages about pro-tecting their children. On the one hand it is very punitive towards them if they don't, but on the other I have seen cases where women whose children have been sexually abused by their fathers have been threatened with contempt by the courts for refusing to allow those fathers access to the children.'

As soon as Ruth realized that her husband had buggered her elder son and sexually abused their two other children, she had absolutely no doubt about what she had to do. 'I was going to protect my kids, come hell or high water, but all the way down the line, people in authority have tried to thwart me.'

First, there was her GP who not only refused to believe her but wouldn't even talk to her children, let alone examine them. Then there was the well-known firm of solicitors who refused to apply for an injunction to prevent her husband from seeing the children – 'They said, "It can all be done through the divorce. There's no need to pillory your husband as a child molester."'

When the divorce went through, they insisted on a form of words in the arrangements for the children that would allow her husband access to them, if they wanted to see him. 'The children didn't want to see him and they kept saying so, because he had always treated them so badly, quite apart from the sexual abuse. In the end I went up to the divorce court myself and, having explained that my solicitors hadn't done what I'd asked them to, asked the judge if she would accept my own handwritten version. But my husband wanted access to the children, so a court welfare officer was sent to see them and make a report. After he'd gone, the children told me he'd talked a lot about them going to visit dad in prison. They'd told him that they didn't want to. They also said they didn't want him to have access to them when he came out, or to have information about their progress, and that they didn't want to have any information about him. As far as they were concerned, their relationship with him was finished.

'In his report he said that the children *did* want access to their father and indicated that I'd tried to influence them the other way. At the access hearing, luckily, the judge wasn't swayed by the report and we got an order for no access to the two younger children. The eldest boy was then over eighteen, so it wasn't relevant.

'What I still can't understand is why professionals behave like this when sexual abuse is uncovered. It seems to me their attitude is that men need to be protected at all costs, and women and children don't matter.'

Although various professionals talked to Ruth's children, they certainly didn't listen to what they had to say – with the exception of the police. The same is true in Sheila's case. No one listened to her daughter Angela, or asked what she wanted, which was to be back with her family again – stepfather included – and for the abuse to stop.

Gerrilyn Smith is acutely aware of how easy it is for professionals unwittingly to repeat the abuse of power by riding roughshod over the child's wishes. 'I think you have to be guided by the child, if in your professional judgement she is old enough. If a fifteen-year-old said to me that she wanted to be back with her family, even if her abuser hadn't admitted the abuse, I would probably let that happen. Even if the decision makes me anxious, it's not my family, it's not my life. If she thinks she can manage the situation, then OK. What is important is that we accept her wishes, but always keep the door open so that she knows she can come back to us at any time. I have seen Care orders used to allow a child to live at home after a period away from the family. It gives her some power, because she knows that if he touches her ever again, she has the force of the law behind her and she can leave.'

With younger children, though, Anne Bannister points to the problems inherent in trying to do what they want. 'They always want the abuse to stop, but for the family not to be broken up. It's like divorce. You ask children what they want and they say, "To live with mummy *and* daddy, and for the rows to stop." It's not possible to give them what they want. My view is that it's impossible to do any work with the child while the abuser is still there, and under our system in this country that usually means removing the child. The child may well say she doesn't want to go, but that is when you have to exercise your power – this delicate balance I spoke of before. Are you doing it purely for the child's protection, or are you using your power for the sake of it? In this instance, I believe it's the former.'

ALTERNATIVES

But many children still view the authorities, in whatever shape or form, as the enemy, and would rather put up with the abuse than actually involve them. For those children, Richard Johnson has developed his own approach to the problem. 'I don't see my job as giving kids the strength to carry on putting up with abuse. I see it as stopping it happening.

'When the kid is ready – and it can take months for a kid to trust me enough to say, "OK, let's do something about it" – I arrange for him or her to leave the house and go to a friend or relative who can be trusted, or to one of our own safe houses. Then, quite simply, I confront the abuser. I phone him up, tell him who I am and what I do, and say that he won't get his child back until we've talked. Then I go and see him.

'Often his first response is to test you out. He'll say, "You know she's a fucking liar, don't you?" Then I get up, shake his hand, and as I walk towards the door I'll say, "See you in court." That never fails. He'll grab my arm and say, "Come on, sit down." Or else he'll threaten to charge me with kidnapping. I give them the phone number of the local police station and the name of the local detective inspector, and say, "Do ring him. He knows me." It's a service no one has never ever availed himself of, for some reason! And then we get the justifications. "She led me on," "She's promiscuous," "I wasn't getting enough from my wife," "I had a rotten childhood myself." I catalogue the events of my own childhood, tell him I have three teenage daughters whom I've never even thought of abusing, and then say, "So what's the next excuse?" Then we get down to the business of getting it sorted out, and getting him off to a shrink or a therapist.

'To make sure he keeps up the treatment and doesn't re-abuse, I threaten him not with violence, but with the fact that I will be on his back. I might arrange that a guy will ring me twice a week at a certain time. If he doesn't, then I ring him. One guy who worked for a government department failed to ring, so I rang his office and told his secretary I was Richard Johnson from Incest Crisis Line and needed to speak to him urgently. He never, ever forgot to ring me again.'

Not surprisingly, many statutory agencies disapprove of ICL's methods, partly because they operate outside the system, but mainly because they are making a presumption about the alleged abuser's guilt. It's a danger that ICL counsellors are aware of, but they make the point that children rarely lie about abuse and that a child would be very unlikely to let them confront her abuser if the allegations were untrue.

Nevertheless, some individual police officers and social workers are happy to work with them because, Richard Johnson believes, ICL is taking away from them a job they really don't want to have to deal with anyway. 'We're now in a situation where some police officers will ring us immediately someone discloses incest. "Before we set this ball rolling," they say, "which we won't then be able to stop, will you come along and see if it really is one for us?" That's brilliant, because – quite unofficially – it builds into the system a flexibility that just isn't there.'

If an abuser won't cooperate, then Richard may have to involve the police or social services, but *never* without the permission of the child. 'If I told without their express permission, then I would become just another abuser. And anyway, it's counterproductive. The child will simply deny that she's being abused and we shall all have lost out.'

The system which most closely resembles ICL's unorthodox way of tackling abuse is the 'confidential doctor' system in Holland. Staffed by part-time paediatricians working alongside social workers, it was set up in 1972 in response to a need for someone with whom concerned adults, neighbours, could share their suspicions about abused children. They work on the principle that the best interests of the child are almost always served by that child remaining in the family, and that their own role should be to help, not punish; so involving the police or the courts in the form of the Child Protection Board is absolutely the last resort. The threat of it is usually enough to ensure the cooperation of an otherwise uncooperative parent.

When a case of suspected child abuse or neglect is reported to the confidential doctor, he will arrange to talk to the child in the company of an adult she trusts, and then to the parents. In one case described by Margaret Jay and Sally Doganis in their book *Battered* (Weidenfeld & Nicolson, 1987), the child in question had been sexually abused by her uncle. Although he was only 'invited' to the confidential doctor's office to face the child and her parents and accept responsibility for what he had done, he knew that if he refused to do so the file on the case would be handed over to the Child Protection Board. He also knew what the likely outcome of that would be. According to one of Amsterdam's confidential doctors, in 90 per cent of cases it is an invitation abusers cannot refuse.

If it is agreed that the child has been sexually abused, then the abuser – who is usually the father – must accept responsibility for it and the mother must believe the child and take her side. They must also agree to undertake a programme of treatment that the confidential doctor devises for the family. He will not be involved in the treatment himself, but will use a wide variety of self-help groups, voluntary agencies and counsellors to provide the help they need individually and as a family.

Appealing though the confidential doctor system is in many ways, it could not easily be transplanted to this country. Our legal system and our fundamental attitude to the roles of the individual and the state are very different, as Jim Christopherson points out in an article in the *Journal of Child Abuse and Neglect* in which he compares the different approaches to sexual abuse here and in Holland:

> The Dutch have a long tradition of intervention by the caring state in people's lives and accept it. The English believe that the individual is the best if not the only judge of his own best interests and see the state as an institution with which he is in conflict.

CRIMINAL PROCEEDINGS

Few cases of child abuse reach the courts in Holland. Many more do here, but even so, a large number of cases never make it to court. The reason is often 'lack of evidence'. Most sexual abuse is not penetrative, so there is seldom any medical evidence. According to the first Annual Report of the NSPCC and Greater Manchester Authorities Child Sexual Abuse Unit, in 51 per cent of the victims there were no physical signs of abuse. Many cases don't come to light for years, never mind months or days, so there is seldom any forensic evidence – semen, blood or hairs – that could identify the abuser. By its nature, sexual abuse is a hidden, secret crime, so there are seldom any witnesses. A 'child of tender years', which in practice means under the age of about twelve, cannot give evidence on oath, and though a younger child can give unsworn evidence provided the judge decides she is of 'sufficient intelligence' and can understand her duty to tell the truth, no one can be convicted on her uncorroborated evidence alone. There has been some argument about what constitutes corroboration. There have been instances where several children 'of tender years' have been abused by the same person and all tell a very similar story. In some cases that has been accepted by the court as corroborative evidence; in others it has been thrown out. The new Criminal Justice Bill will do away with the need for corroboration of evidence given by a 'child of tender years' but the prosecution will still have to prove its case beyond reasonable doubt. Just because such evidence will be admissible, there is no guarantee that it will be believed.

As we saw in Chapter 1, the view is still widespread, despite all the evidence to the contrary, that children at best fantasize, and at worst lie, about these things. There is also a feeling that children are unreliable witnesses in that they are easily led and can't remember accurately what happened several years ago.

Recent research here and in the USA has found this simply isn't the case. Previous studies showed that children were good at recalling some particular event they had witnessed, but one group of American researchers wanted to see how well they would remember some distressing event in which they were themselves involved. They therefore videotaped a group of children between four and seven while being vaccinated. A week later they were questioned and although they were asked misleading 'leading questions', they remembered the main event clearly.

One year later, the children were cross-examined by pairs of lawyers and the videotapes shown to juries who were told they were witnesses in cases of medical negligence. The children's memories were remarkably consistent on the central events of vaccination day, though it had faded on peripheral things, such as how many chairs there were in the room. They were not influenced by misleading 'leading questions' this time either. That is the good news. The bad news is that most of the jurors tended not to believe the children, especially the younger ones, although in fact one four-year-old had been the most accurate of all. So what is clearly needed is not simply a change in the law but a fundamental change in attitudes.

Many children whose cases have been prosecuted through the courts might be forgiven for thinking that those whose cases were dropped for lack of evidence were the lucky ones. For some children, having to stand in the witness box only feet away from their abuser, surrounded by strangely dressed people, mostly male, being cross-examined by a defence barrister in exactly the same way as an adult witness would be, is an experience almost as bad as the abuse itself.

When Rose's husband stood trial in Scotland for abusing her eight-year-old daughter, she asked if she could sit close to her – not close enough to whisper, but close enough to give her moral support. 'In the event, I was made to go and sit right at the back of the court, and the Procurator Fiscal stood between us so that she couldn't see me at all. The only person anywhere near her was her stepfather just feet away in the dock, with his eyes fixed on her face, and she sat there sobbing. At one point the court was cleared on a technicality and I was made to go out, and I could hear her through the doors, crying, "Mummy! Mummy!"'

Rose's daughter was not a good witness, but at least Rose had actually walked in on the abuse and so was able to testify. And indeed her husband had once abused her nine-year-old niece as well. 'Before the trial we were all very worried about my niece because she kept dissolving into tears. But once she got into the witness box she was so strong and fierce that my husband actually had to look away from her in the end. She was so strong in fact that the judge construed it as proof that the abuse hadn't harmed her at all and so that wasn't taken into account in the sentencing. It seems that we prefer our victims to be weak and pathetic, but not too pathetic in case they break down in the witness box!'

Some research is under way, funded by the Home Office, into the legal system's treatment of children as victims of crime (to be published in September 1989), and tentative steps have already been taken towards making the trial itself less of an ordeal for a child. After the outcry last year when a nine-year-old girl broke down in the witness box and the judge was forced to acquit three adults accused of abusing thirteen children, screens were introduced at the Old Bailey for the first time, so that the children didn't have to look at their alleged abusers. In the Criminal Justice Bill, there is a clause which would allow the use of live video links so that a child under the age of fourteen can be cross-examined from a room away from the court-room itself. But this will only apply to Crown courts, not to magistrates' courts where some sexual abuse cases are heard, and will be at the court's discretion. And quite how it will work no one yet knows. Will the prosecuting and defence counsels be in the room with the child, and if so, how can the accused communicate with his counsel? Will the child be cross-examined by disembodied voices from the court-room or by lawyers and others on a video screen?

Some people believe these changes are not radical enough and would like to see a videotape of the child's original disclosure admissible as evidence. Not only would the child's recollections be fresh, but it would protect her from the ordeal of having to tell her story over and over again. In June 1988, the Home Office announced the setting up of an enquiry under Judge Thomas Pigott into the possible use of such recordings in court hearings. Under the new law concerning child sexual abuse introduced in Canada on 1 January 1988, such videotapes are admissible, but there are problems. One condition is that they must be made within 'a reasonable time' of the abuse, but many children don't disclose for years. It is also true that children rarely tell the whole story on one single occasion – they often disclose a little at a time over a period of weeks; so how many videotapes would be admissible? And then there is the problem the Great Ormond Street team has encountered (though in their case it was with transcripts of videotapes). Their primary motivation in an interview with a child is diagnostic and therapeutic. It is not to collect evidence acceptable in a court of law. When subsequently transcripts were asked for by the courts, some were criticized on the grounds that the children had been 'led'. There is concern that, if such videotapes are permitted as evidence, the people conducting the interview would have that fact in their mind and so the interview would not be as beneficial to the victim as it ought to be.

There is also considerable opposition to the use of such video-tapes in this country from people who believe that a fundamental principle of British justice – the right of the defendant to cross-examine witnesses – would be undermined. The suggestion that the videotape could be admitted as evidence and the child then cross-examined on matters arising from it, rather than having to tell the whole story yet again, is greeted with no greater enthusiasm.

One use of such videotapes has proved successful in some parts of the USA and in this country in the London Borough of Bexley. A tape of the child's disclosure has been shown to her alleged abuser and his solicitor, and in a number of cases the accused person has changed his plea from 'not guilty' to 'guilty'. 'You'd have to be a really tough nut to see the child actually disclosing what happened,' said Detective Chief Superintendent Anthony Kilkerr, who is in charge of the Metropolitan Police initiative on child sexual abuse, 'and still say the child's lying.' Not only does that spare the child the ordeal of appearing in court, but – just as important for her long-term recovery – the abuser publicly accepts the responsibility for what happened.

However, given the way our legal system works at present, there is very little incentive for an abuser to plead guilty. For one thing, his lawyer will tell him how difficult such cases are to prove, and that there is always a chance that the child will break down in the witness box, as happened in the notorious case at the Old Bailey, so that the judge will be forced to dismiss the case. Even in another recent case where 'genetic fingerprinting' showed that the odds against a twelve-year-old girl's stepfather *not* being the father of her baby were over *25 million* to one, he chose to plead not guilty just in case there was a technical hitch in the trial.

Most people who either plead or are found guilty of sex offences against children are sent to prison; given the extremely rough time sex offenders are given in prison, few men are going to volunteer for that. In the Great Ormond Street study, of those found guilty, 71 per cent went to prison (8 per cent of them for less than one year, 42 per cent for between one and two years, 31 per cent for between three and five years, and 8 per cent for more than five years; the length of sentence served by the remaining 11 per cent isn't known), 14 per cent were given suspended sentences, about 10 per cent were put on probation, and in the case of one man treatment was ordered. It is possible for courts to make probation orders with a treatment condition attached, which means that the man has regularly to attend either one-to-one sessions with a named psychiatrist or psychologist, or a group session. If he doesn't turn up, it is a breach of his probation and he will find himself back in court. But such orders are few and far between because there simply isn't sufficient skilled help for offenders.

A DIFFERENT APPROACH

In some parts of the USA the problem is tackled by means of 'treatment diversion programs', such as that in Santa Clara, California.

When sexual abuse in a family comes to light, the professional, volunteer and self-help elements involved in the Child Sexual Abuse Treatment Program (CSATP) move into action. The family may need immediate support during the crisis, as well as long-term treatment programmes for all its members. Although some fathers are discouraged by their lawyers from starting treatment right away, before their case comes to court, on the grounds that this could be construed as an admission of guilt, the CSATP professionals can usually convince them that it is in their clients' best interests. The fact that an abuser is already in the CSATP when the case comes to court works in his favour, and his continued participation in it is usually a condition of his probation or parole. It is very rare for a CSATP client to be sent to prison; the worst that happens is a few months in the local rehabilitation centre, from which he can usually carry on working and attending his counselling sessions and group meetings. Most offenders are given a suspended sentence or, increasingly, an order to devote several hundred hours' work to Parents United, one of the self-help groups in the programme.

It is by no means a soft option. For many it is hard and painful work to come to terms with what they have done, genuinely accepting responsibility for it and changing the way they treat not only their children but their wives. Some people would argue that any change achieved with the threat of a prison sentence hanging over your head can't be genuine change, but the achievements in Santa Clara speak for themselves. In the first ten years there were no reports of re-abuse among the 600 families treated. Other US studies on recidivism in incest families showed rates of between 2 and 20 per cent; and it is worth noting that most of those were carried out on offenders who had been sent to prison, the majority of whom did not return to their families, whereas 85 per cent of the offenders in the CSATP did.

In other parts of the USA, the diversion into treatment comes even earlier in the process. In return for making a full statement confessing his guilt, which could be used in a court of law, an abuser can go on to a treatment programme and the case will not go to court at all unless he drops out of treatment or re-offends.

Dr Arnon Bentovim at Great Ormond Street feels strongly that such a system would be the best way forward in this country for first offenders in cases where there is no violence and where the abuser takes responsibility for what he has done. Officially we have no treatment diversion programmes in this country, but in effect that is what former probation officer Ray Wyre is running for child sex offenders in Hampshire.

'What happens is that I have now got clearance from the Law Society to prepare court reports on offenders, and where the level of offending is high enough to warrant a condition of treatment in any probation order, I put the treatment programme into the report. The court then decides whether to accept my proposals or not.

'About 40 per cent of the men I'm now working with would have been in prison if it hadn't been for the programme – some of them for a very long time. One man, who had raped an eight-year-old girl and is on the programme for sexually assaulting his ten-year-old nephew and having sex with a girl of thirteen, would have probably gone down for at least ten years. The probation officer was convinced he would re-offend within weeks, and the judge shared her concern to the extent of asking for quarterly reports on his progress. It's over a year now, and he hasn't re-offended. Nor have any of the others.'

In the summer of 1988 Ray Wyre set up a residential clinic in the Midlands funded by a private nursing organization, where offenders will stay for up to two years and where he plans to use a whole range of therapies. Because it is residential, he hopes to be able to take offenders charged with even more serious offences.

He, too, is convinced that treatment diversion programmes are the way forward. 'The system as it is now creates denial because we don't offer offenders any incentive to confess. At the moment the only pay-off for coming clean is prison. The moment you offer a diversionary programme in an area, even if they can't get on it, guys are more honest in the hope that they can. I have had guys ringing their solicitors from my office to change their plea to guilty because there's a chance they might be able to come to me.'

6 *Help*

There seems little doubt that the best immediate help for any sexually abused child, once the abuse has been disclosed, is to be believed, supported and in no way blamed by her parents, or, if the abuser is her father, by her mother. But in many instances, especially if the abuse is within the family, the disclosure comes as such a crushing blow and the mother is so overwhelmed by her own anger, guilt, disgust and pain that she can't give the child all the support she needs. Equally, if the abuse has been going on for years, there are already such problems within the family that the mother hasn't the inner resources to cope. In that situation – and indeed sometimes even when a child is supported and believed by her parents – she needs help.

Ray Wyre, who has wide experience of working with victims as well as abusers, really does believe that a stitch in time saves nine. 'If you can get to children soon enough and put the message across that they weren't to blame for the abuse, then I don't think it takes long-term, heavy counselling to sort it all out. What you can do by acting quickly is prevent them from writing a "life script" in which they cast themselves as victims – that's what creates long-term problems.'

Although some extremely interesting and valuable work is being done, most concerned professionals agree that there simply aren't enough facilities to cope with the demand. In those areas where there is a treatment programme there are often long waiting-lists, and in other areas there is nothing at all.

Paula feels very angry that they were offered no help after her daughter disclosed that her grandfather had abused her. 'There are so many people encouraging children, and adults, to "come out" with their abuse, but when they do there is no one there to help pick up the pieces. Yes, there is a sense of relief in telling your story and being believed, but, for me anyway, that was momentary. After-wards you have to work through all those buried feelings that you've dredged up, and there was no one concerned with helping me to deal with that.'

In some cases, children are referred to child psychiatrists or clinical psychologists for help, but in cases where a child had been abused within the family, many treatment programmes like those at Great Ormond Street or Guy's Hospital, or various NSPCC projects up and down the country, take the view that you can't help a child in isolation. The abuse happened within the family, and so the family needs help too.

A range of different treatment methods are used in these pro-grammes. Individual therapy is offered to all family members, in-cluding other children in the family who may not have been abused but who are not unaffected by what has been happening. They may have been very jealous of the attention shown to the abused child, without of course understanding the reasons for it. They may blame the abused child for the upheaval at home when the abuse is disclosed, and resent the fact that everyone in the family is so weighed down with their own problems that no one has any time for them. For small children, the sort of activities used in helping them disclose are very valuable therapy too. Play of all kinds, working with dolls and puppets, drawing, modelling, enable them to express the feelings they can't put into words. In a safe environment, being able to yell in rage or punch and kick the doll who has been labelled 'daddy' or 'grandpa' without fear of any repercussions can give a child a tre-mendous sense of relief. As we briefly mentioned in Chapter 5, art and play can also be therapeutic for older children, and, because they are more articulate, so are more traditional forms of therapy.

Anne Bannister is a great believer in the virtues of psychodrama for children and adults. 'You can work through the same sort of things that people work through in psychoanalysis, only more quickly, because you don't have to have a logical thought process. People who aren't very bright intellectually can do it just as well as people who are, because it's about feelings, not thoughts, and I don't think there are hierarchies of feelings.

'As we know, it's nature's way to make us repeat traumas in order to try and make sense of them. Psychodrama does the same thing but in a safe place, with people who will not re-abuse you. It's better than just talking about it, which doesn't always get you into the feel of it. Our bodies remember what our minds forget, so you need to do bodily things to recreate the feeling of a situation. If a woman has been raped and gets herself into the position she was in when it happened, she will feel what it was like.

'Once you have got yourself into the feeling of the experience again, someone trained in psychodrama can help you work through it. We tend to think what happens to us is our fault, and that we could have done something differently. Not so. In psychodrama you can see very clearly that you didn't really have any options, so you can work through the feelings of guilt and discover where the guilt really lies.'

There are groups, too, for abused children of different ages (Great Ormond Street, for example, has mixed groups for 3- to 6-year-olds and 7- to 10-year-olds, groups for younger and older teenage girls and a group for teenage boys), for mothers, for parents, and – in some places – for abusers. Simply being in a room with other people who are in exactly the same situation can be very helpful in breaking down the sense of isolation, the secrecy, the shame, the feelings of responsibility for what happened that most victims and many mothers feel. The sharing of experiences and feelings and the mutual support are common to most therapeutic groups, but the Great Ormond Street team point out that theirs also have very specific goals in terms of education and changing behaviour – teaching children how to protect themselves against abuse in the future, for instance, and helping mothers to protect their children.

Apart from being beneficial in their own right and as part of a wider therapeutic programme, groups also have an obvious advantage where resources, both in terms of professional skills and money, are scarce. You can simply help larger numbers of people that way.

A British-born doctor, John Denison, was instrumental in setting up a programme for abused children in the York region of Ontario, Canada, which has become a model for the whole state. 'Realistically, on a cost-effectiveness basis, group therapy offers the best "dollar value" for money and effort expended. This doesn't preclude the individual services that are certainly needed, but it demands careful planning and management of available resources.' He also says that it has been a long, hard slog over the last twelve years to establish a programme that meets the needs of local communities on the spot and not at a large regional centre miles away. What's more, the whole venture would not have been possible without the huge contribution made by volunteers. Without them, he maintains, the professionals would simply be incapable of coping with the scale of the problem. They work not only in essential support roles – administration, driving, fund-raising – but are also trained as group leaders. 'There's a two-week initial training period with talks by knowledgeable group leaders and other experts, followed by a nine-week minimum "on-the-job" training period, working alongside an experienced leader in a group. The volunteers are then assessed on their ability to lead a group, and if the assessment is positive, they are taken on. So far, it is working very well.'

As well as group work, some programmes in this country also work with 'dyads' – pairs – within the family, such as mothers and daughters, to help resolve the problems peculiar to that particular relationship. A mother may not have felt as close to the abused daughter as to other children in the family and, when the abuse is disclosed, blames her as much as she blames her husband. If the family is to be reunited, the social workers or doctors concerned must be certain that the child will be protected in future, and acceptance by the mother that the child is not to blame for what happened is a key element in that. Others work with the mother and her abusing partner to try and tackle the problems in their relationship, which, although they are not the cause of the abuse, were a factor in allowing it to start and to continue.

Most programmes also offer family therapy, which, put simply, brings all the members together in an attempt to help them recognize those malfunctions in the way the family operates which made it possible for the abuse to happen, and, in time, to put them right.

Take, for example, a family where the mother and one of her daughters have exchanged roles – because the mother has become ill, or is overburdened with too many children, or has been treated like a child by her husband – so that the daughter has not only become the father's sexual partner but is also responsible for organizing the household, disciplining the younger children, and so on. There, the aim of family therapy would be to re-define the necessary, proper boundaries between parent and child, help the parents assume parental roles again, take the burden of responsibility from the child and encourage her to relate to her brothers and sisters as one of them and not as a substitute parent, and vice versa.

Although all the programmes of treatment are 'child centred' in that they put the child's interests first and treat the other members of the family in order to help her, there are differences in emphasis. Families on the Great Ormond Street programme will usually be attending the relevant groups, possibly having individual counselling, and taking part in family therapy concurrently.

Anne Bannister works intensively with victims, with their mothers, with any brothers and sisters, and hopes that someone else will work with the abuser; she believes that family therapy at the start of treatment is a waste of time. 'I am often accused of not understanding what family therapy is, but I did it myself for years in my work as a probation officer. What it does very well is to change the dynamics of a family, but we believe that is just treating the symptoms, not the disease, which I see as the basic power structure in the family. You need to inject against the disease first, if you like, and then, if the symptoms persist, tackle them by bringing the whole family together and looking at the dynamics.

'Family therapists, by implication, take the view that you can't really attach blame, and that the problems arise from the way people interact with each other. We believe that in child sexual abuse there is one person at fault, and that's the abuser. O K, there can be lots of reasons why they have done it, but it is their fault it has happened, and that must be totally accepted by everyone. Only then can you try and put the family back together. In my experience family therapy doesn't often work. It's not surprising. If you give treatment to all those people, you hope they are all going to change, but when you put the pieces back together again, the fit will probably be wrong. More often than not families split up when child sexual abuse has occurred, but I don't think that is necessarily a bad thing, because people can recover and exist in a different kind of family.'

Richard Johnson agrees. 'If someone had said to me as a kid, "Guess what? Tomorrow we're all going to the hospital and dad will be brought in to talk to you", I think I'd have opened a vein. I would like to see much less emphasis on reconstituting families, because the nuclear family as the be-all and end-all is an outmoded concept, and more emphasis on what the kids want.'

To be fair, many children do want their families back together again, dad and all, but if that were the sole aim of family therapy – which it isn't – then Great Ormond Street's figures suggest that it isn't particularly successful. Of the couples in their study, 18 per cent were separated, 4 per cent were in the throes of divorce and 26 per cent were divorced, when the follow-up was done between two and five years after treatment had ended. At the beginning of treatment, though, the majority of families were described as stable; 57 per cent had been together for five years or more, and 29 per cent had been together for over ten years.

'My own view on why families break up, despite periods of relative stability before that,' said Dr Bentovim, 'is that it is partly because, in the sample we were reporting, there had been a good deal of imprisonment, and we know this leads to family break-up. Also it may very well be that the abuse of the child was maintaining a false sense of togetherness, and the moment matters came into the open it produced a tremendous explosion.' But it would seem from other findings that the break-up of the parents' marriage is not necessarily a bad thing for the children.

The professionals working with families in the community were asked by the team to assess the overall situation of the victims as a result of treatment. They thought that 61 per cent were better off, 24 per cent had stayed the same and 10 per cent were worse off. (The issue of whether or not they had been abused again was dealt with separately; 16 per cent had been re-abused, in the case of 15 per cent it wasn't clear whether they had or not, but in 69 per cent of cases there had been no further abuse.)

As for adults who were sexually abused as children, there is very little official help on offer. Some women do receive therapy, it is true, but usually only because their own children have been physically or sexually abused. Most of the help available to adult victims is through voluntary agencies.

For many women, rape crisis centres are the first port of call. Some are extremely good and will either counsel the women themselves or refer them to someone else who will. Others take a fiercely feminist line. 'It is a problem for us,' says Valerie Howarth of ChildLine, 'to know where we can, with confidence, refer adult victims. One woman rang at one a.m. one morning. She'd just watched "Childwatch" on television and had told her husband for the first time about her experiences as a child. They were ringing to ask where she could go for help. A woman like that, who is happily married and needs to try and make sense of her childhood experiences, doesn't need to be told that all men are rotten and have nothing more to do with them.'

Male victims often get very short shrift. Richard Johnson is still very angry about one thirteen-year-old boy. 'He had been raped by his father and was bleeding from the anus. He ran out of the house on a freezing cold night with only a shirt on, and rang the local rape crisis centre from a phone box. They told him to fuck off because he was male. When I rang a local rape crisis centre down here to try and get help for my niece, Annie, they simply hung up on me. When my wife rang back and asked why, they said it was because I was a man. We eventually found out about Incest Survivors' Group (now defunct), but when Annie contacted them they said they'd help her but not her twin brother, whom her father had also abused, because they didn't help men.' He was eventually given a number for Incest Crisis Line, got in touch, and as well as getting help for Annie, he was himself recruited to train as a counsellor.

Incest Crisis Line now have nine lines around the country, handling on average 1,500 calls a week. They will help anybody who has been the victim of sexual abuse, past or present, male or female. They also have secondary counsellors with whom victims can be put in touch if they want help face-to-face.

All their counsellors have themselves been victims of sexual abuse. This is something that a few professionals regard as a considerable disadvantage, partly because, they would argue, people who haven't yet sorted out their own problems are not in the best position to help others in trouble, and partly because their own experience gives them a false sense of their own expertise. They may know how it was for them, but that doesn't mean they know how it is for every other victim of sexual abuse. But for many victims, simply being able to unburden to someone who knows from first-hand experience exactly what they're talking about can be remarkably therapeutic.

Richard Johnson doesn't believe in asking many questions. 'I ask their first name and suggest they make one up if they feel more comfortable. I ask their age at the onset of abuse, the last time they were abused and how old they are now. I also say that I will never ask them what their dad or whoever did to them. It's none of my business. If they choose to tell me, that's fine, but I get really cross with some of the creeps around who say, "You must talk it through. Until you talk the actual incidents through you're never going to deal with it." That's voyeurism.'

Anne had to drink almost a whole bottle of vodka before she could make her first call to ICL. 'God knows what this bloke must have thought. There was this drunken woman, rambling on and crying and swearing. I must have been on the line for hours that night. I did that a couple of times, but eventually I got around to calling when I was sober, and it was just extraordinary to be able to talk about what had happened to me and not to feel – as I'd always done before when I'd tried to tell friends – that they were angry with me because I was giving them something they didn't want to hear.'

When Anne became confident enough to meet other women in the same situation, she discovered that Sue lived within five minutes' walk of her flat and they became close friends in a very short time. 'We don't talk about our past a lot because we don't need to. But it's just great being with someone who knows without being told why you suddenly go quiet, or why you don't want to talk one day. You're not frightened that you're going to let something slip out and see that familiar look of disgust on someone's face.'

Richard Johnson and his fellow ICL counsellors believe it's a very important step on the road to recovery for victims to confront their abuser, if only by letter, when they feel ready. Sally felt so confident and strong about confronting her father that she decided to phone him rather than write a letter. 'It was in the middle of the Cleveland inquiry, and I read something in the paper about a psychiatrist who was supposed to have said that sexual abuse could be enriching for a child. I flipped, and for three weeks I walked around in a daze, totally unable to do anything, let alone pick up the phone and call my father. Finally I sat down and wrote him a letter, setting out exactly what he had done to me and to my life. I told him he had to contact Richard Johnson, and when he did, Richard told him he should write back to me, taking responsibility for what had happened and apologizing. He did that, but, interestingly, his reply didn't matter to me. Writing the letter myself was the important step. As I dropped it into the post-box, there was a great sense of a weight being lifted off my shoulders. I haven't responded to his letter, nor to the one after it saying that my mother was really worried about my silence and that I shouldn't blame her. It's a problem, not knowing if she knew or not. If she did, it's simple – I don't want to see them again. If she didn't, then I don't want her to know. I don't want revenge. I just want them to get on with their lives and leave me to get on with mine.'

Paula also confronted her father by letter – addressed quite deliberately to his business address so that her mother need not know. 'When I posted the letter – basically I wanted him to admit what he had done to me, to apologize and give me an assurance that it wouldn't happen to my own two daughters or my nieces – I had a terrific sense of relief. Next day, real fear overwhelmed me because I knew my father was a very powerful man and I didn't know what would happen as a result. A few days later, my husband and I received a typed letter from my father saying that my letter had been put into the hands of his solicitor, and the contents of it had been made known to my mother, my sisters and brother-in-law, all of whom had read his letter too. He went on to say that if I wished to destroy him I would never succeed. He signed it, and so did my mother, but with her full signature, not as "Mum". He'd won again, and I lost my family. One of my sisters wouldn't speak to me for months, and said I was insane . . . I realize that I lost nothing, that I had nothing there worth losing, but I did grieve . . .'

Childwatch, the Hull-based charity founded by former social worker Dianne Core in 1985, also offers telephone counselling to sexually abused children and their parents. Meg, whose son Christopher was abused by the local parish priest, doesn't know what the family would have done without Dianne. 'Even after a year, talking to Dianne on the phone seems to be the one thing that makes Christopher feel any better. He's been seeing a psychiatrist, but after ten minutes or so he just doesn't want to talk about it any more. He doesn't talk to me much about it, and if he does I just cry.'

ABUSERS

As has already been said, many people get very heated at the idea that any public money should be spent on treatment for men convicted of sexually abusing children. All the resources available should be devoted to the victims, they argue; they refuse to see that trying to stop abusers re-offending when they come out of prison is actually one way of protecting other potential victims. But in fact they don't have a great deal to get heated about. The Home Office has no central policy on the treatment of offenders and where it happens, it happens in an *ad hoc* way. Psychiatrists may see some prisoners individually, and in a few prisons where sex offenders tend to be concentrated, probation officers run groups. Some work is being done using behavioural techniques like covert sensitization, in which the abuser is asked to describe his illegal deviant fantasies, followed by fantasies of something he finds highly aversive. The process is repeated and he is then offered a fantasy 'escape scene' – something that is sexual but legal.

Grendon, the experimental prison in the Midlands with a therapeutic regime for some inmates, takes a number of sex offenders, although it also houses other types of prisoner. Originally the whole prison was run on therapeutic lines, but as a result of prison over-crowding it now takes some young offenders who are not on the special regime. But according to Ray Wyre, who has worked in a number of prisons, the approach in Grendon, which is basically psychoanalytical, isn't particularly effective with sexual abusers because it doesn't get past the barriers of denial, justification, minimization and so forth that abusers build around themselves.

Some prisoners elsewhere may be given drugs, at their own request, to reduce production of the male hormone testosterone. Although these do have some side-effects, they are nothing like as serious as the side-effects of the female hormones which used to be given to male sex offenders, such as growing breasts which had to be removed surgically.

In 1988, a 27-year-old paedophile who had sixteen convictions for sexual offences against boys was the first patient to be treated at his own request with an anti-cancer drug, Goserelin, one of the side-effects of which is to suppress sexual urges. After the treatment had been stopped by the Mental Health Act Commission on the grounds that he hadn't given informed consent, he appealed to the High Court to reinstate it.

But for many offenders, prison offers little or no treatment. 'We had a weekly session with the prison doctor,' said Peter, 'but it was general chit-chat, not any attempt to tackle the real problems. I did ask to see the doctor privately to try and find out why I had done what I'd done, and we fixed an appointment a few weeks ahead. When the day came, he said, "Can't help you. You're being moved to another prison. I'll put a note on your file that you want to talk to someone," and that was that. I never did get to see anyone.'

Like most sex offenders, Peter spent most of his sentence on 'Rule 43' – segregated from other prisoners for his own protection. 'Most other prisoners on Rule 43 are sex offenders too, so it's a relief to be able to talk about what you're in for – something you simply daren't do on the ordinary side of the prison. But you are so protected in there that when you come out your nerve has gone and you jump at the slightest noise.'

What concerns Ray Wyre is not simply that most men get no treatment, but that they are locked up for twenty-three hours a day with other sex offenders, exchanging ideas, contacts and fantasies, masturbating and reinforcing the patterns of behaviour that put them inside in the first place.

Tom, for example, recalled sharing a cell with one man a few years ago. 'He talked to me a lot about young girls, what he did to them and where to find them. After I came out, I met him again and wound up having sex with his twelve-year-old daughter. That's what I got done for the last time.'

When men are released from prison, some may be able to return home if their wives, and the social services, permit. Under a new directive, the local authority has to be notified before anyone who has abused a child can return to a home where children are living. (Before, the local authority had to be notified only when the abuser had already abused a child in the home to which he was planning to return.) But what tends to happen is that decisions about a possible return home are not made until the man is released, and only then is any necessary rehabilitation work started. While the decision is being made – and, of course, if it has already been decided that he cannot return home – he has to find somewhere to live.

'When offenders are released,' Ray Wyre points out, 'they are not supposed to mix with other ex-cons, so those that have no homes to go to are dotted around bed-and-breakfast places. Who are the other main group in bed-and-breakfast? Single-parent families! God knows how often single mums have asked one of these nice kind guys to babysit!'

There is now a certain amount of help available to abusers outside prison. Men in the Great Ormond Street programme are sometimes allowed to attend family therapy sessions from prison, and there are a few groups getting underway to help abusers after they have been released, or in some cases as a condition of their probation orders. Four members of the NSPCC's child protection team in Rochdale started their first group last September and are about to start another in the autumn of 1988. Dr Eileen Vizard is running a group in Newham, east London, and Ray Wyre's group in Hampshire has been going for over a year at the time of writing.

Although they work in slightly different ways, all are agreed about the major problems involved in working with abusers – the layers of denial, justification, minimization and 'normalization', which run very deep.

Dr Vizard recalls going to assess one man, on remand in prison and charged with sexually abusing his two daughters, as a potential member of her abusers' group. 'He said that of course he was perfectly well aware that the abuse was his responsibility, and was outraged that I'd even asked the question. We talked some more, and he described how his seven-year-old daughter often came downstairs in her nightie for a cuddle and wriggled around on his lap, which he found arousing. I asked him to what extent he thought the children played a part in what had happened. He said immediately, "Well, obviously they played some part in it. They can't go wandering round the house half naked without expecting something to happen, can they?" I asked him to what degree he thought they'd played a part – 5 per cent? 20 per cent? 50 per cent? He said, "About 20 per cent."

'You are dealing here with a split perception. Intellectually he knows it's his fault. But emotionally he feels that the child led him on or did something that made it her fault and not his. Denial is pretty deep-seated and, realistically, in terms of treatment you are talking about years rather than months.'

With his group, Ray Wyre spends a lot of time working on 'cognitive distortion' – the distorted view of their activities that all abusers have. The nature of the problem very soon becomes clear as they talk.

First, there is the minimizing ('I only did this . . .' 'It was just a bit of fondling . . .') and the justification ('She wanted me to go the whole hog, like' – 'she' being a child of nine, and he, a man in his sixties). Tom was furious because one of his sisters told the family that he had molested a four-year-old: 'I've never ever gone below the age of seven or eight and I never will!' He was also deeply offended that the police had roped him in for questioning after the rape of a sixty-year-old woman in the area. 'I said to them, "What do you think I am? Desperate?"'

Then there is the normalizing ('A doctor in the paper says it can be very enriching for children to have a sexual relationship with an adult'), and the denial. 'I know I'm meant to say the whole thing's 100 per cent my fault,' said Ken, whose conviction for incest was discussed in Chapter 3, 'but it carried on for so long and it seeemed to me she clearly wanted it as much as I did that I still can't believe that she wasn't partly to blame.'

When a new member joins Ray Wyre's group, he is put on the 'hot spot', and the other members, as Ray puts it wryly, check out the reality of the statements he makes. 'He can't hide anything from the other group members because they have all been there and they know. I've got guys who can break down denial in two minutes flat. They take the guy outside for a minute and that's it. Exactly what they do to him I don't know – there are never any marks! But it works.'

The fact that the group has been running for over a year means that newcomers have to face a well-established group ethic. According to Eileen Shearer, one of the workers in the NSPCC's group in Rochdale, the lack of such an ethic, inevitable in a group that is starting from scratch, has presented problems. 'We started by getting each member to tell the group in detail what they have done, and encouraged the other members to challenge them. But some of those who hadn't yet had their turn colluded with the man in the hot seat, making excuses for him and so on, in the hope that when it came to their turn they'd have an easy time of it too. We're hoping that with the new group, by including some of the members from the original group, it won't happen again.'

Another crucial element in Ray Wyre's work with the group is 'victim awareness' – making group members realize that the children they abuse are damaged by the experience. 'It's very important, especially with paedophiles who are convinced that they love children and do them no harm. A number of men in the group were themselves abused as children, and we use their experiences as victims to show the paedophiles that they actually do a great deal of damage.

'We also look at re-victimization. Paedophiles take advantage of children who have already been sexualized from previous abuse, and think that's OK because they weren't the first. You try and make them see that, in a way, it's worse. It's bad enough that a child has been abused once, but for it to happen again reinforces the child's "life script" of herself as victim.

'The one type of offender I would not have in a victim aware-ness group is a sadistic killer or rapist. The trauma they cause is part of their arousal system, so the last thing they need to be told is just how serious the damage they do can be.'

Peter, who went to prison for incest and for sex with under-aged girls, found the victim awareness sessions very painful indeed. 'I never thought what I was doing harmed the girls. I got into the way of thinking that when new girls came round they knew exactly what they were in for, because the others would have told them. I gave them money, drinks and cigarettes too, so I really thought it was all right. Even after I came out of prison, I'd see some of them in the street. Some would smile, others would ask when I was going to start again! Again, I didn't think I'd harmed anybody. After the sessions with Ray, though, I didn't sleep for days. It became painfully clear to me that those girls were victims – my victims – and I am really dreadfully sorry for what I've done.'

Ray Wyre's approach to his clients is actually very different from most social work or therapeutic approaches. For one thing, he always assumes, and lets his clients know it, that he knows all about them. 'Ask a sex offender if he's ever offended before, and he will say, "No." If you say, "How many other offences have there been? Sixty? Seventy?" he'll say, "Not that many – fifty, maybe."

'I was asked to do a report recently on a guy in prison. A psychiatrist had seen him for ten minutes and wrote in his report that this was a one-off offence against his two grandchildren, he was not obsessional and unlikely to re-offend. The probation officer wasn't happy with it, and asked for a report from me. It turned out that the man had been a paedophile since his teens, is obsessional and was masturbating up to four times a day in prison to a fantasy of his girlfriend and her child in bed with him. But if you ask questions like "Have you done it before?" or, worse, "You haven't done it before, have you?" or "Do you think you might do it again?" or "Do you masturbate?" you'll get predictable answers.'

Another way in which his approach is very different is that he doesn't trust his clients. 'I say to them, "I don't trust you bastards an inch", and they accept it. If you hand trust out like lollipops, they'll think you are incredibly naive and will con you till the cows come home. I don't believe words; I believe behaviour. I tell them, "The best predictor of future behaviour is past behaviour, and until you demonstrate to me through your life that you are changing, that's what I'll stick with." So they know I don't trust them, but they know that I care.'

In over a year, no member of the group has re-offended, but even so, Ray finds more reason for pessimism than optimism. 'The more you get to know these guys, the more you get inside their heads, the more dangerous you realize they are.'

He is also concerned about the long-term future of the group. He can't go on for ever – other abusers need his help. 'They want to carry on, but I'm sure that without a worker there to keep challenging them, it will just turn into a paedophiles' circle.'

The scale of the problem daunts him sometimes – the sheer numbers of abusers and of abused children – but he believes there is no alternative but to carry on. 'I don't have an intrinsic love for sex offenders – indeed I would grass them up to the police at the first opportunity if I found they had re-offended – but it's vital for child protection to get as much information as we can from these guys. It's important, too, to stop them offending again for as long as possible, to prevent another child from being victimized.'

In the vast majority of cases, the sexual abuse of children is a cycle of behaviour that goes on repeating itself not only through the abuser's own lifetime, but possibly through his children's, and his grandchildren's. In terms of human misery alone, when you think of the appalling damage that can result from child sexual abuse, it makes sense to try to break that cycle by tackling the problem at source. When you consider the vast number of social problems that result, it also makes economic sense. At the moment, though, in terms of the sheer scale of the problem, the resources devoted to treating offenders are hopelessly inadequate. In this respect, too, they are right at the bottom of the heap. This parsimony is extremely short-sighted. Surely the question should not be, 'Can we afford to treat abusers?' but 'Can we afford *not* to?'

7   *Prevention*

No matter how much money the government or local authorities or charities spend in trying to pick up the pieces, trying to repair the damage done by child sexual abuse, it can never be enough. Given that prevention is not only better than cure but is also almost always a whole lot cheaper, this is an area where more resources should be targeted.

Of course, you can never ensure that every child is completely safe from paedophiles. As Bill, who has abused around 200 children, put it, 'You tend to go for unhappy, neglected kids, but even normal kids can be got at by a determined paedophile.' And he should know. You can't protect every child from abusing parents, either, but that's no reason not to try and protect as many children as possible.

Some people argue that protection programmes for children are a bad thing in that they deflect attention and, by implication, some of the responsibility from the people with whom it belongs, the abusers, to their victims. To focus on what children should and shouldn't do implies that their actions invite abuse. The same argument is used about women and sexual crime. Why should women be told not to go out alone late at night? It's not women who rape men, after all. Philosophically that argument is irrefutable, but it is of little practical use to a child in trouble.

However, there is a good deal that parents can do to help protect their children, much of it very simple, basic commonsense. For a start, they can spend more time with them. Ogden Nash summed it up very neatly: 'One would be in less danger/ From the wiles of the stranger/ If one's own kin and kith/ Were more fun to be with.' As Ray Wyre has discovered, what makes many paedophiles so successful in their contacts with children is that they are prepared to give them a lot of time and attention.

Parents can also check out the adults (and older children) with whom their children come into contact. Babysitting is a case in point. How many parents quite happily go out, leaving their children with the teenage son of a friend of a friend? And what's more, leave with the order, 'Now you do exactly what he tells you, or there'll be big trouble!' There are a significant number of cases where children have been abused by teenage babysitters.

Ideally, you should only leave your children with someone you know well – another mother, or a relative, though children have been abused by grandfathers, uncles and cousins, too. For that reason it is very important to note a child's reaction to the news that a particular person is coming to babysit. If they are upset or distressed, then try to find out why, and *listen* to what they say. Michele Elliott, co-founder and Director of Kidscape, quotes the case of an eight-year-old girl who said she didn't like her uncle because he 'teased' her. Her mother told her that everyone has to learn to put up with teasing, but a few weeks later the child was found to be suffering from gonorrhoea of the throat. Had her mother pursued the remark about 'teasing' and why the child disliked it, she might have been able to stop the abuse going that far.

Ray Wyre believes that most parents' quite understandable ignorance of the way in which paedophiles operate leads them to be far too trusting. 'If a 45-year-old man, with no apparent expressed sexuality – no girlfriends *or* boyfriends – wanted to take my fourteen-year-old son off to concerts or sporting events, I would be very suspicious. But many parents wouldn't even ask themselves what this middle-aged man is getting out of forming a friendship with a fourteen-year-old boy. Maybe it is all perfectly innocent; maybe I've been working in this field too long; but it's not a risk I would be prepared to take.'

It is important that you should have as open a relationship with your children as possible so that they can feel free to tell you anything without your being shocked or furiously angry. The parent has yet to be born who wouldn't be angry when a child admits she has done something she's been told a dozen times not to do, but try to keep the anger in proportion and avoid the temptation to say 'I told you so' when the consequences you have always predicted follow. It may mean that the child will be afraid to tell you if she has broken some rule – come home alone, for example – and has been molested as a result.

It is also very important to encourage children to set boundaries for themselves from a very early age – and to respect them. You can't teach a child that her body belongs to her and then insist on scrubbing her ears with a flannel while she struggles and protests. The message you are then putting across is that her body belongs to her unless someone bigger and stronger decides for whatever reason, that it doesn't.

Psychotherapist Jenner Roth found a very interesting example in her own family. 'We used to tickle our son, and sometimes he would enjoy it but then it would go too far, he'd find it unbearable, and become angry with us. Then we began to find he was bugging his father all the time, and we realized that the same thing was happening – we were saying "no" and he wasn't listening, just as he said "no" sometimes when we were tickling him, and we weren't listening. So we made a contract that whenever anyone in the family says "Stop", we stop. It's hard to stick to sometimes, but it is important to teach a child that his "no" is valid.'

That raises a fundamental issue in the whole question of teaching children to be strong, to stand up for themselves, that parents have to face. If you are going to teach them that it's OK to say no to an adult who wants them to do something they don't want to do, they are going to say no to you sometimes, too. Although older children will no doubt try it on, they will be able to see that there is a real difference between your request to be in at a certain time, or clean up their room, and, say, an invitation by an adult acquaintance to go to his home and play video games. But with younger children it's much more difficult. If it is going to be effective as a means of protecting them, they have to believe deep down that they do have the right to say no. If you start to whittle away at that right with all sorts of exceptions, they are not going to believe in it and it won't work. You can't, for example, tell them it's all right to say no to strangers, but not to adults they know. Between 50 and 75 per cent of children are sexually abused by adults they know. You can tell them they have the right to say no to an adult who touches them in a way that makes them feel uncomfortable, but you can't then insist that they kiss grandma when they don't want to, or get angry if they protest loudly when a family friend pats them on the head and messes up their hair.

Jenner Roth believes that parents quite unconsciously undermine children's self-respect and autonomy in little ways all the time. 'Why do we force them to eat things they don't like, for example? And especially why do we make them eat things they don't like before they can eat something they do like? The message there is that in order to get rewards they have to do unpleasant things, and that of course is a very common pattern in child abuse: "Do as I say and afterwards I'll buy you a present." What I'm talking about, I guess, is a seditious upbringing – raising bolshie kids who won't do it just because you say so. But given that children who are abused are often those who have been taught that authority is always right and who always do as they're told, that's a price I personally am prepared to pay.'

In the experience of Michele Elliott, the price doesn't have to be that high. 'We have done follow-up studies with 4,000 parents whose children have been "Kidscaped" at school. Those studies showed that children's attitudes towards affection – family cuddles and kisses – hadn't changed, which some critics thought they would, and that children weren't frightened by the programme. Although most of them were more assertive, they weren't unruly.'

Since we have all become so much more aware of child sexual abuse, many schools all over the country have responded in a variety of ways. Some have dealt with the subject themselves, devising their own programmes. Others have invited outsiders, such as the police, or a charity like Childwatch, to come into the school and talk to the children. Almost 2,000 primary schools use the Kidscape programme (the under-fives version is on its way, followed by one for the group aged eleven plus) devised by Michele Elliott, herself a teacher and educational psychologist, and Wendy Titman, after long and careful research. Michele Elliott explains: 'I started out to run the programme in schools myself, but I soon found that I had a list of almost a thousand schools waiting, so the only way was to devise a programme schools could use themselves.'

Designed for use by teachers, it covers every aspect, from setting up a 'parents' evening' to show them what the school plans to do, and getting their permission for their children to attend, to the lessons themselves.

'It's very important to remember that the majority of children aren't sexually abused, thank God, so you mustn't scare children to death,' said Michele Elliott. 'One commercial video I've seen ends with a small girl in bed, looking very frightened, with the shadow of a man – either dad or the lodger, it's not quite clear – looming over her. That is a very powerful image and I know from what parents have told me that it has frightened some children a lot. I am very opposed to the use of videos in this area, anyway, because they are passive. It's essential that a child's introduction to the subject is interactive, a dialogue between child and teacher.

'Kidscape also deals with sexual abuse – two words we never use, incidentally – in the context of other things. It's not singled out, it's tackled along with other frightening, potentially dangerous situations, like getting lost or being picked on by bullies. I really do believe it's not necessary to destroy children's innocence to make them safe.'

Indeed, if parents do object to their children being taught anything with a specifically sexual connotation – that they have a right not to be touched on their private parts, for instance – the programme is designed to work just as well with those sections removed.

The lessons usually start with the teacher asking the children to describe situations in which they feel safe – being tucked up in bed at night, for example, or having a cuddle with mum. They then move on to think about situations in which they wouldn't feel safe – being lost, being in the house by themselves, and so on – and how they might deal with them.

Children are taught that what grown-ups tell them to do isn't automatically right and that they don't always have to obey. The teacher asks them to imagine what they might do if she told them that they could never eat again, couldn't go home after school, or even told them to stop breathing!

Through stories or role-play, they explore unpleasant or even potentially dangerous situations: being bullied; being approached by a stranger; being subjected to inappropriate kisses by an uncle, and being told to keep it a secret. They are told that hugs and kisses should *never* be a secret and that if anyone suggests they should be, the child should tell an adult they trust. This also applies if anyone tries to touch them in a way that makes them feel frightened or confused. They learn to say no, and that if a stranger approaches them, it is not rude to walk, or run, away and not to become involved in conversation. They learn how to yell in a deep, low voice (not to scream, because most adults would simply think that was just children playing and ignore it). They also discuss how to tell an adult – mum, in this instance – what's been going on.

As Michele Elliott says, there is no way of proving how effective Kidscape is because you couldn't have two groups of children, one who had been Kidscaped and one who hadn't, expose them to exactly the same real danger and compare the results. But the anecdotal evidence that comes pouring in is enough to make her believe that the programme is on the right lines. 'Very recently a mother phoned me about her eleven-year-old son, who had been through the programme at school. He had been walking home from school when he saw two guys coming towards him with knives. He had yelled, run round them, and carried on running to the police station about two hundred yards away, where he was able to give the police a good description of them. He went home and didn't even mention it to his mother. The first she knew was a call from social services, who had been contacted by the police, and who asked if her son needed help in coping with the trauma he had just suffered. When she asked him why he hadn't said anything to her, he just said, "Well, I've been Kidscaped. It was no problem."'

Where sexual abuse is concerned, the programme seems to work in two ways. First, it enables children to say no at the first approach and to tell someone right away. Michele Elliott gives an example: 'One teacher told me that an eight-year-old girl came to her and said that her teenage brother had come into the bathroom while she was in there and had tried to wash her between her legs. She had said no, loudly, and though she was too scared to tell her mother, she did tell her teacher and they were able to tell the mother together.

'It seems that Kidscape also enables children who are being abused to tell someone about it for the first time. In one county where all the primary schools are using the programme, there have been over fifty disclosures from children who were being abused. Again, there is no way of proving categorically that they felt able to do that as a result of Kidscape. But we did look at two schools of similar size, one of which had used the programme and one of which hadn't. In the former there were forty disclosures; in the latter there were none.'

Michele Elliott is well aware that Kidscape isn't like an inoculation – one shot and you're protected for ten years, if not for life. It's a message that must be repeated again and again for it to become second nature. Various research projects have shown that although children take in the messages clearly at the time, they do fade. In one study the children were quite clear, soon after the programme, that people you knew, as well as strangers, could do you harm, and that strangers didn't necessarily look weird; they looked like everybody else. But six months later, when they were asked again about people who harm children, most said they were strangers, and weird-looking ones at that.

In an ideal world, personal safety, like road safety, should be a regular part of every school's curriculum, not a special lesson every now and again. It isn't allowed for in the new core curriculum which Kenneth Baker's Education Act will bring in over the next few years. It will have to fight for time, along with a host of other subjects, in the half-day a week not accounted for by the core subjects. But if parents feel strongly enough about it, then perhaps they will be able to exercise the 'parent power' which the government insists is at the heart of its new bill, and make sure the time is found.

But we can't leave the entire responsibility for children's safety to the schools. Obviously parents, individually, have a vital role to play, but so does the community at large. There have been suggestions that we should set up 'safe houses', as has been done in some parts of the USA and Australia, which display a special sign and to which children in trouble know they can go. Both Dianne Core of Childwatch and Michele Elliott feel that, although the suggestions are well motivated, the problems involved in checking out the adults in such houses to make sure the children really would be safe are insurmountable. Paedophiles are often extremely plausible and not at all easy to identify, as the organizers of children's helplines have discovered to their cost. Michele Elliott is also concerned that if on the one hand you tell children to avoid strangers and keep clear of unsafe or uncertain situations, you are contradicting yourself if you then tell them to run into a stranger's house just because it has a sticker in the window.

What we *can* do is keep our eyes and ears open, and if we suspect a child is in trouble, we can tell someone. Where physical abuse is concerned, we are now much better at contacting the NSPCC or the social services than we once were. It's harder with sexual abuse because it rarely leaves physical marks, but as public awareness increases and we learn the signs to look out for in our own children, and in any other children we come across, we must share our suspicions with someone. It's not easy to do. We as a nation are brought up to mind our own business and not to interfere, but that is exactly the attitude which allows child sexual abuse to flourish.

SYMPTOMS

The following symptoms are often displayed by children who are being sexually abused. The fact that children display one or even two of them does *not* automatically mean that they are being abused. But if they display a number of these symptoms, and there are no other valid explanations for them, it's worth investigating the possibility of sexual abuse.

Physical symptoms

Chronic itching or pain in the genitals.
A recurrent vaginal discharge or cystitis.
A sore bottom.
'Tummy' pains that have no physical cause.

Bedwetting.
Nightmares; a reluctance to go to bed; difficulty in sleeping.

Eating problems: overeating; loss of appetite. Anorexia nervosa in older girls.

General behaviour

Aggressive behaviour and tantrums.
Becoming overly compliant.

Becoming clinging/insecure.

Adopting a 'don't care' attitude.

Becoming isolated from friends; trusting no one.

Reverting to outgrown patterns of behaviour – wanting a bottle, for instance or discarded cuddly toys.

A sudden change in academic performance in school; an inability to concentrate.

A sudden urge to wash or bath a lot.

A sudden loss of trust in a familiar adult and an unwillingness to be with him.

Self-destructive behaviour: suicide attempts; running away; self-inflicted wounds; drinking or taking drugs.

Sexual behaviour

Talking about sexual matters excessively and in a way that is inappropriate for the child's age.

Continual overt masturbation.

Playing explicitly sexual games (ordinary games of 'mums and dads' or 'doctors' are usually not a cause for concern).

Reacting to adults in an inappropriate sexual way.

8　The Cure?

Long before the Cleveland crisis had even begun there was a growing awareness that the response of all the concerned agencies to the rapidly increasing numbers of diagnoses of sexual abuse among children was inadequate. In April 1986 the Department of Health and Social Security (DHSS) published draft guidelines for all agencies involved in child-abuse work in a paper called 'Working Together'. As its title suggests, it stressed the importance of inter-agency co-operation and stated that investigations into child sexual abuse require 'a particularly high level of co-operation between social services departments or the National Society for the Prevention of Cruelty to Children and the police and doctors'. It also made the point that cases of suspected abuse need social as well as medical assessment. 'Medical evidence alone is frequently inconclusive when seen in isolation but may help to provide a clear picture of abuse when seen in conjunction with social evidence.' The paper stated, somewhat radically in the light of attitudes that are still widespread, that a child's disclosure of abuse 'should be accepted as true until proved otherwise'.

But even in 1986, in some areas, the level of co-operation between the various agencies was already good, and in a few areas joint initiatives were under way. In 1985 the Metropolitan Police and Bexley social services, for instance, had set up a pilot training scheme in which social workers and police officers were trained together in joint interviewing techniques. Although this initiative sounds relatively straightforward, it actually involved major shifts in attitude on all sides. Senior police officers had to accept a change in priorities. As Detective Chief Superintendent Anthony Kilkerr, chairman of the Met's Child Abuse Working Party, says, 'If you like, we pushed policing to the bottom of the list. Our first priority became the protection and welfare of the child, our second priority the rehabilitation of the family, and our third priority dealing with the offender.'

Those being trained had to overcome their mutual suspicions and antagonisms. To social workers the stereotypical policeman is fascist and macho. To policemen the stereotypical social worker is a 'basically left-wing, namby-pamby do-gooder'. As one detective constable put it, 'In general social-work views are entirely opposed to police views. Their job is to do good. We're not interested in doing good; we're interested in solving crime and putting the villain up in the box.' As well as lectures from a variety of experts, the course included self-awareness sessions. In one session the group was divided into pairs, one social worker and one policeman; each had to describe a personal sexual experience in detail, while the other had to ask questions to solicit more information. The aim was to make them aware of how difficult it is for adults, never mind children, to talk about such an intimate experience. Although they all found it extremely hard, they also found it very valuable in terms of breaking down barriers. In the words of one group member, 'After you've shared that, everything else is easy!'

The subsequent experiment in joint investigations was felt to be such a success that the Bexley project has provided a starting-point for schemes to be set up throughout the Metropolitan Police area over the next two years, though the fact that of the forty London boroughs only five are wholly contained within one of the eight police areas means that negotiations with social services departments will be complicated.

According to the Social Services Inspectorate report commissioned by Health Minister Tony Newton at the same time as the Cleveland inquiry, seventy-one areas out of 118 in England and Wales accepted the principle of joint working, but only twenty-two had set up joint training schemes. In other areas the majority of local authorities reported generally satisfactory cooperation with the police in cases of child sexual abuse, though there were twenty-nine areas where the police and social services had no agreed policy to consult each other before undertaking investigations. Because of the judicial inquiry set up at the same time, Cleveland itself was excluded from the Social Services Inspectorate report. Had it been included, the inspector would no doubt have come to the same conclusions as Lord Justice Butler-Sloss, who stated in her report: 'In general we were satisfied with the arrangements and the interdisciplinary working of the main agencies in Cleveland in their response to child abuse *other than to child sexual abuse* [my italics].' It is the analysis of the very unsatisfactory state of those arrangements in relation to sexual abuse that occupies most of the Cleveland inquiry report.

THE CLEVELAND REPORT

The long awaited, much leaked and much speculated-upon *Report of the Inquiry into Child Abuse in Cleveland 1987* (Cm 412) was finally published on 6 July 1988. People who had hoped for simple answers, for the guilty men – and women – to be named and for the whole distressing affair to be neatly resolved were disappointed. It was a complex response to an extremely complex problem, enabling people to find in it what they wanted to find.

The tabloid press, which had decided from the start that Dr Marietta Higgs was the villain of the piece, saw no reason to change their minds. 'Not a sign of regret' was the *Daily Mail*'s headline, alongside a photograph of Dr Higgs smiling. *Today* used the same photograph with the headline 'Condemn this laughing crusader', implying that Dr Higgs's reponse to the report's findings was to laugh. Before the report was published much of the media coverage focused on the 'innocent families' caught up in the Cleveland crisis (as though somehow the *families* in which children had been abused were 'guilty') and the suffering of parents. The same was true of much of the tabloid and television coverage immediately after the report was published. Few articles or programmes made any reference to the plight of the children in Cleveland who had been sexually abused.

It was an oversight of which Lord Justice Butler-Sloss was determined not to be guilty. 'The children in Cleveland' (both those who were abused and those who were not) are the first group to be dealt with. In Chapter One of the report she states, 'In the rest of this Report we set out the events and the responses of the adults which from time to time may appear to be entirely centred upon adult perceptions and concerns, and the arguments which surrounded them seemed to have little to do with the problems of the children themselves. In this chapter we have set out the impressions and perceptions of some children during the crisis in an attempt not to fall into the same trap.'

The report then tells, briefly, the stories of twenty-one families in which the children were diagnosed as being sexually abused and the outcome. In two cases in which the children had been made wards of court the judge held that they had not been sexually abused, so they were dewarded and returned home. In two further cases the children were dewarded with the consent of all parties involved. In two other cases, in which the children concerned had both disclosed sexual abuse, the police found insufficient evidence for proceeding with a prosecution (see page 9). In one case a ten-year-old girl was returned home even though she had revealed that her father had abused her and had actually asked to be taken back into care; in the other, the child eventually went to live with an aunt. In all the other cases either someone (a father, a stepfather, an uncle) was prosecuted for sexual abuse or the court felt that the balance of probability was that the children concerned had been sexually abused, so they remained either wards of court or in the care of the local authority. The *Daily Mail* chose to report just two cases – in both of which the judge decided the children had not been sexually abused. Of the fifteen cases in which the courts found evidence that the children had been sexually abused there was not a mention.

The tabloids also made much of the fact that ninety-eight of the 121 children made wards of court or removed from their families under Place of Safety orders or care orders have returned home. None of them mentioned the fact that although twenty-seven of the sixty-seven children who were made wards of court went home with all proceedings dismissed, a further twenty-four went home under supervision orders or on conditions as to medical examination, and two went home under interim care orders. (The report does not make clear under what conditions, if any, children who were removed from home but not made wards of court and who are now back home were returned.) Of course, that is not to say that all those children were definitely the victims of sexual abuse, but it suggests that the courts were sufficiently concerned that abuse was a possibility to keep a watchful eye on the children.

The Report's Main Findings

The bulk of the report is devoted to the causes of the Cleveland crisis of 1987, to charting the lack of cooperation, and the breakdowns in communication, not only between the agencies concerned – social services, the health authorities, the police – but also between individuals. 'Professional priorities and values were forgotten as the inter-agency squabble became increasingly personal. The interests of the children became completely submerged.' No group escapes criticism in the report.

Drs Higgs and Wyatt are both criticized for not examining their own actions, not considering whether their practice was always correct or whether their actions were in the best interests of children and their parents. They are also criticized for 'the certainty and overconfidence with which they pursued the detection of sexual abuse in children referred to them'. The report does go on to say, however, 'In all this we must not forget that some children seen by Dr Higgs and Dr Wyatt had been sexually abused.' Their reliance on reflex anal dilatation (see page 29) is also criticized. Dr Higgs, the report says, came to rely on R A D as 'diagnostic rather than raising suspicion and requiring further investigation'. But the report also makes clear (again, something one would not have learned from many newspapers or television documentaries) that although 'in the opinion of the Inquiry the sign of "reflex anal dilatation" was given undue weight by the paediatricians' medical examinations, in only eighteen out of 121 cases was it the sole physical sign and in *no case was it the sole ground for the diagnosis*' [my italics]. Lord Justice Butler-Sloss went on to add that while both doctors bore some responsibility for the events in Cleveland, 'it would be an unjust over-simplification to place the whole burden of the crisis upon the shoulders of Dr Higgs and [Dr Wyatt]. There were many other contributing factors to the crisis.'

Sue Richardson, Cleveland social services' child-abuse consultant, is criticized for advising that immediately a diagnosis of sexual abuse was made by the doctors, a Place of Safety order should be sought and the child removed from home, without ensuring that the wider assessment that social workers ought to make in sexual-abuse cases was always undertaken first. Social services managers are also criticized for 'naïveté' and for failing to reassess what they were doing in the light of a sudden increase in the incidence of child sexual abuse. One minor criticism of social workers, but interesting none the less, was that they had removed children from foster homes in which they had been placed as a result of suspected sexual abuse on the grounds that they had been further abused in the foster home. The report states that this ought to have raised questions in the social workers' minds about the validity of the initial diagnosis. 'The fact that foster parents have been through a selection process which would have involved making careful inquiries into their backgrounds and the taking of references does not seem to have weighed with social workers in deciding how they should respond . . .' While I have no doubt that social services departments screen prospective foster parents as carefully as possible, it is painfully clear from the example of Bill (see pages 61, 64), who was on the books of several fostering agencies and reckons that he abused over 100 of the children he fostered, that it is extremely difficult to screen out a 'successful' paedophile who has managed to avoid detection and prosecution. (One Cleveland mother whose child was correctly diagnosed by Dr Higgs as having been sexually abused had not known until then that her own husband was a Schedule 1 offender – in other words, a convicted child abuser.)

The report attributes responsibility for the breakdown in rela-tions between social services and the police to both agencies. Police surgeon Alistair Irvine 'got out of his depth. He found himself placed in the position of medical adviser to the Cleveland Constabulary, and did nothing to extricate himself. His strongly held views and emotional behaviour did not help a situation which required a calm, cool, dispassionate evaluation of the problems. He bears a measure of responsibility for the troubled relationships between the Police and the Social Services department, and the lack of balance in some of the media coverage.'

The Chief Constable and the Director of Social Services, Mike Bishop, are also held responsible for failing to 'understand the depth of the disagreement between their staff and as a consequence failed to take some joint action to bring their two agencies together'.

While the Inquiry accepted both the need of a Member of Parliament to represent the interests of his constituents and that it was entirely proper that what had been happening in Cleveland in 1987 should have been made public, the Labour MP concerned, barrister Stuart Bell, who took up the parents' cause, was criticized for his 'intemperate and inflammatory remarks', such as his comparison of events in Cleveland with seventeenth-century witch-hunts, a comparison he elaborated on in the title of his book on the Cleveland crisis, *When Salem Came to the Boro*, published in July 1988. As Professor Anthony Clare pointed out in a review of that book, it is clearly an inadequate analogy, since, unlike witchcraft, child sexual abuse frequently does occur. A number of Mr Bell's allegations –'empire building' by social services, for example, and 'conspiracy and collusion' between Drs Higgs and Wyatt and Sue Richardson to keep the police out of child sexual abuse cases – were carefully examined by the inquiry, and no evidence was found to support them. In his own evidence to the inquiry, Mr Bell agreed that there was no further evidence on which he was relying to support such allegations, and Lord Justice Butler Sloss concluded, 'We were sad that he was unable, in the light of the further knowledge that he clearly had, to withdraw or modify allegations which could not be substantiated.'

The Recommendations

Having explored in great detail what went wrong and why, the report states its determination that what happened in Cleveland should not be allowed to happen again and, to that end, makes a number of recommendations. First of all it stresses the need to recognize and describe the extent of the problem of child sexual abuse and to collect more accurate information about it. It suggests too that more research is needed into symptoms associated with sexual abuse and into RAD particularly. It also stresses the importance of seeing a child as 'a person and not an object of concern'. Professionals should explain what is happening to the children, listen to them and, in deciding what to do, take their wishes into consideration. They should not subject them to repeated medical examinations (the children from one family in Cleveland were examined no fewer than seven times) or to repeated interviews.

Parents should be kept informed and should be consulted at

every stage. Social services should seek to provide support for them; they should not be left feeling isolated and bewildered, as many Cleveland parents were. Parents should be allowed to attend case conferences unless their presence would prevent a full and proper consideration of the child's interests. Place of Safety orders should be sought only for the minimum time necessary for the protection of the child, and parents should be given information about their rights in clear, comprehensible terms. If children are taken into care, arrangements for access should be made unless there are 'exceptional reasons' not to do so. In such cases social services should tell parents about the avenues of complaint or appeal open to them.

As for the agencies involved – social services, health authorities and the police – the report recommends clear structures for monitoring what is going on and stresses the importance of good inter-agency communication and cooperation: each agency should acknowledge that 'no single agency . . . has the pre-eminent responsibility in the assessment of child abuse generally and child sexual abuse specifically'. To this end the report recommends the setting up of Specialist Assessment Teams, consisting of a senior social worker, a doctor and a police officer, to make an assessment of the child and the family in cases in which there is strong suspicion of sexual abuse but no clear evidence. One of the major needs exposed by Cleveland, the report states, is training at all levels for professionals involved in child sexual abuse. (Psychiatrist Tony Baker estimates seventy-two different professions may be involved, from magistrates to marriage guidance counsellors.)

The report also gives its backing to the Government White Paper on reforming child-care law, published in January 1987, particularly the proposals to replace Place of Safety orders with eight-day emergency protection orders, under which the courts could decide whether parents' access should be terminated and whether a child should be medically examined if the parents withhold their consent.

At the end of the report Lord Justice Butler-Sloss raises a number of points for 'further thought and wider discussion'. She suggests, for instance, that to avoid removing a child from home while suspicions of sexual abuse are investigated, social services could use some of their budget to pay for alternative accommodation for the suspected abuser. She also stresses the need to recognize the problems of adults who disclose childhood abuse (see Chapter 2) and the lack of help available to them at present. She raises too the question of whether diversionary programmes of some kind might be considered for the type of abuser who 'may wish to confess to the abuse but is inhibited from doing so by fear of the consequences' (see page 129). Her last suggestion is the setting up of an Office of Child Protection to scrutinize local authorities' applications in care proceedings and ensure that they are well founded, to call for additional investigations and to invite local authorities or the police to think again about instituting civil or criminal proceedings.

THE GOVERNMENT'S RESPONSE

Health Minister Tony Newton, speaking for the government in the House of Commons, welcomed the report. He announced that the government would introduce, as soon as possible, legislation based on the 1987 White Paper on child-care law reform, including the replacement of Place of Safety orders by eight-day emergency protection orders, which will include the right of parents to challenge such orders after seventy-two hours if they have not been involved in their granting. He announced that the government would make available £7 million for training, provided that local authorities themselves found a further £3 million to bring the total to £10 million (a sum that the Labour spokesman, Robin Cook, felt was inadequate; he pointed to the government's failure earlier in 1988 to find the £40 million needed to increase social workers' basic training from two years to three and to the fact that by 1992 Britain would be the only European country in which social workers received only two years' training). Mr Newton also announced that before the end of the parliamentary session the Lord Chancellor would issue a consultation paper on the feasibility of setting up an Office of Child Protection.

Guidelines to all professionals working in the field of child sexual abuse were published at the same time as the Cleveland report, the findings of which formed an important part of them. An updated version of the DHSS draft guidelines 'Working Together' was issued, stressing the need for close inter-agency cooperation and for balanced assessments based on all the strands of evidence.' It emphasizes that social services departments must give 'first and highest priority to protecting the child. However, they also have responsibilities in relation to the child's parents and other family members or carers.' Whereas the first draft of the guidelines said, 'A child's statement that he or she is being abused should be accepted as true until proved otherwise,' the updated version, modified on the advice of the Royal College of Psychiatrists, states, 'A child's statement about an allegation of abuse, whether in confirmation or denial, should always be taken seriously. A child's testimony should not be viewed as inherently less reliable than that of an adult.' (In fact, the only witness to present evidence to the Cleveland inquiry on the question of false allegations was an American psychologist, Dr Underwager, who stated that 65 per cent of allegations of sexual abuse turned out to be false. Other research that suggests that children, particularly young children, seldom lie about sexual abuse – see page 28 – was not presented.)

Separate guidelines for doctors on the diagnosis of child sexual abuse were issued by the DHSS's Standing Medical Advisory Committee (SMAC). They state, 'It is no longer reasonable for any doctor to expect never to see a case of [child sexual abuse] and all doctors should consciously raise their awareness of the subject.' They make the very important points, largely overlooked in all the arguments about the presence or absence of certain physical symptoms, that physical signs do not occur in every case in which serious and/or long-standing sexual abuse is actually taking place and that no one physical sign (including RAD) can be regarded as being 'uniquely diagnostic of CSA', although the presence of sexually transmitted diseases, unsurprisingly, gives rise 'to a high index of suspicion'. They also state that if a doctor has reason to believe that a child is being physically or sexually abused, 'not only is it permissible for the doctor to disclose the information to a third party, but it is a duty of the doctor to do so'. That takes no account of views of the Official Solicitor – who represented the children's interests at the Cleveland inquiry – concerning a child's right to confidentiality. He said that a child should be told to which agencies a finding of sexual abuse was likely to be reported – police and social services, for example – and the likely consequences of intervention in family life and that 'such a child should be entitled to say that such information should be disclosed in a limited way or not at all even though that will preclude anything other than appropriate medical care'. There is a danger that the S M A C's advice, far from preventing the creation of 'double victims' (children who are abused by a perpetrator and again by the system when the abuse comes to light), which the report's recommendations set out to do, in part at least, will actually allow it to continue.

The Home Office has published, for police, guidelines stressing the importance of cooperation and communication with other child-protection agencies. The Department of Education has issued guidelines for teachers, which confirm draft guidelines issued last year, recommending that one senior teacher in every school in the country be trained in detecting sexual abuse and made responsible for co-ordinating the school's response to it. 'Samantha', the one victim of sexual abuse whose evidence was printed in full in the Cleveland report, made the point that there should be several such teachers in each school; if there were only one teacher to whom abused children could turn, a child might be unwilling to approach him or her because other children in the school would guess what the child wanted to talk about.

WHAT HAPPENS NOW?

Overall, the Cleveland report was well received as a cool, balanced look at a very complicated subject, but for some people – Cleveland parents, local M Ps and some newspapers – it was too balanced. They wanted the blame placed squarely on the shoulders of individuals – Drs Higgs and Wyatt, Sue Richardson and, to a lesser extent, the Director of Social Services, Mike Bishop. There have been calls for them to resign or, failing that, for them to be sacked. Some parents have issued writs for damages against the doctors and Cleveland County Council, and Stuart Bell, M P, has launched an appeal to meet their legal costs.

The future of the doctors, both of whom returned to work in March 1988 – Dr Wyatt is at Middlesbrough General but is forbidden to deal with cases of sexual abuse, and Dr Higgs is working in Newcastle with new-born babies, her other paediatric speciality – is to be considered by a special committee of the Northern Regional Health Authority, though it has stated firmly that it will not be rushed into any snap decision. Cleveland County Council has set up a working party to examine the criticisms made in the report and to decide the future of Sue Richardson (who spent most of 1988 away on study leave) and Mike Bishop. Its chairman has said there would be no witch-hunt but no cover-up either.

It is easy to see the appeal of an outcome that lays all the blame for what happened in Cleveland on 'over-zealous' professionals and urges the concentration of resources and commitment in the future on ensuring that parents are never falsely accused again. Such an outcome allows us to tell ourselves that child sexual abuse rarely happens, that it is just the figment of a few well-meaning but misguided professionals' imagination; we do not have to address the fact that, as the Cleveland report states, child sexual abuse is, and long has been, a widespread and deep-rooted problem in society.

The dilemma is not just that many people find the whole subject so repellent and distressing that they simply don't want to think about it; it is also that there are no easy answers. We know the appalling damage that sexual abuse does to its victims. We know that the effects of that damage are often passed on through generations. But what do you do when the victim wants the abuse to stop but loves her abuser, doesn't want him sent to prison and certainly doesn't want to be whisked away from her family herself? How do you balance the damage done by removing her from the only security she knows with the damage done by leaving her where she is but at risk of further abuse? According to many people working in the field, the mere fact that abuse in the home has come to light is seldom enough to stop it, and it is also true that abuse usually escalates. It may start with 'a bit of fondling', but it rarely ends there.

The report, and the various guidelines published with it, offer plenty of advice about investigating suspected cases of abuse and dealing with the immediate consequences of a positive diagnosis. But they are less helpful when it comes to the long-term consequences of child sexual abuse. As a point for further consideration the report raises the possibility of diversionary treatment for abusers. So do the DHSS guidelines 'Working Together': 'Developing ways of providing treatment and rehabilitative services within the legal framework is a major task for inter-agency cooperation. It may be that a treatment and management plan for a known abuser and his family can be achieved by cooperation between all the relevant agencies, thus avoiding a total family break-up (for example, a father being required to live away from home, but accessible to and supporting the family during therapy).' But the point is also made that such an assessment 'must necessarily include consideration of whether appropriate resources are available locally'. And, of course, in the vast majority of places they simply are not.

That is not to say that solving the problem of child sexual abuse is simply a matter of money. If only it were that simple! But certainly to provide the necessary therapeutic help for abusers and for victims, at whatever stage they may need it, will require a large injection of cash. In a political climate in which public spending is regarded as something to be reduced, not increased, however, extra money is unlikely to be forthcoming.

Besides, at the heart of the problem are our attitudes – male attitudes to sexuality and power, and adults' attitudes to children. A child, as Lord Justice Butler-Sloss says, is a person and not an object of concern. She could usefully have added 'or an object for the gratification of adult desires'. Those attitudes are not going to change overnight, and probably not within a generation, but that's no reason for not making a start. A first step would be to stop pretending that the family is always a safe haven for a child and to admit that in child sexual abuse we have a very real problem.

Useful Addresses and Telephone Numbers

ChildLine
> 0800 1111 (calls are free).

Childwatch
> 04302 3824.

Family Network Helplines (run by the National Children's Home)
(London) 01-514 1177
(Scotland) 041 221 6722/3/4
(Wales) 0222 29461.

There are a number of other local Family Helplines; ask Directory Enquiries, or ring 01-354 2337.

Incest Crisis Line
01-422 5100 (Richard)
01-890 4732 (Shirley)
01-593 9428 (Kate).

There are other local lines. Any of these counsellors will put you in touch with your nearest one.

NSPCC (National Society for the Prevention of Cruelty to Children)
The NSPCC offers a whole range of local services. Either ask Directory Enquiries for your nearest branch, or ring:
> (London) 01-404 4447 or 01-242 1626
> (Belfast) 0232 240311.

The Royal Scottish Society for the Prevention of Cruelty to Children
> 031 337 8539/8530.

OPUS (Organization for Parents Under Stress)

OPUS runs a number of local helplines, often jointly with Parents Anonymous. For your nearest one, either ask Directory Enquiries, or ring 01-263 5672 or 01-645 0469.

Rape Crisis Centres

The Centres may be able to offer counselling, or they can refer you to any local groups for incest survivors or victims of sexual abuse. For the nearest to you, ask Directory Enquiries, or ring:

(London) 01-837 1600
(Scotland) 041 221 8448
(Wales) Incest Survivors Helpline 0222 733929.

Kidscape

For information on schools using the Kidscape programme and/or a free leaflet for parents on how to protect their children, send a large stamped addressed envelope to:

Kidscape
82 Brook Street
London W1Y 1YG.

Index

FOR THE BEST IN PAPERBACKS, LOOK FOR THE

In every corner of the world, on every subject under the sun, Penguin represents quality and variety – the very best in publishing today.

For complete information about books available from Penguin – including Pelicans, Puffins, Peregrines and Penguin Classics – and how to order them, write to us at the appropriate address below. Please note that for copyright reasons the selection of books varies from country to country.

In the United Kingdom: For a complete list of books available from Penguin in the U.K., please write to *Dept E.P., Penguin Books Ltd, Harmondsworth, Middlesex, UB7 0DA*

In the United States: For a complete list of books available from Penguin in the U.S., please write to *Dept BA, Penguin, 299 Murray Hill Parkway, East Rutherford, New Jersey 07073*

In Canada: For a complete list of books available from Penguin in Canada, please write to *Penguin Books Canada Ltd, 2801 John Street, Markham, Ontario L3R 1B4*

In Australia: For a complete list of books available from Penguin in Australia, please write to the *Marketing Department, Penguin Books Australia Ltd, P.O. Box 257, Ringwood, Victoria 3134*

In New Zealand: For a complete list of books available from Penguin in New Zealand, please write to the *Marketing Department, Penguin Books (NZ) Ltd, Private Bag, Takapuna, Auckland 9*

In India: For a complete list of books available from Penguin, please write to *Penguin Overseas Ltd, 706 Eros Apartments, 56 Nehru Place, New Delhi, 110019*

In Holland: For a complete list of books available from Penguin in Holland, please write to *Penguin Books Nederland B.V., Postbus 195, NL–1380 AD Weesp, Netherlands*

In Germany: For a complete list of books available from Penguin, please write to *Penguin Books Ltd, Friedrichstrasse 10 – 12, D–6000 Frankfurt Main 1, Federal Republic of Germany*

In Spain: For a complete list of books available from Penguin in Spain, please write to *Longman Penguin España, Calle San Nicolas 15, E–28013 Madrid, Spain*

A CHOICE OF PENGUINS AND PELICANS

The Informed Heart   Bruno Bettelheim

Bettelheim draws on his experience in concentration camps to illuminate the dangers inherent in all mass societies in this profound and moving masterpiece.

God and the New Physics   Paul Davies

Can science, now come of age, offer a surer path to God than religion? This 'very interesting' (*New Scientist*) book suggests it can.

Modernism   Malcolm Bradbury and James McFarlane (eds.)

A brilliant collection of essays dealing with all aspects of literature and culture for the period 1890–1930 – from Apollinaire and Brecht to Yeats and Zola.

Rise to Globalism   Stephen E. Ambrose

A clear, up-to-date and well-researched history of American foreign policy since 1938, Volume 8 of the Pelican History of the United States.

The Waning of the Middle Ages   Johan Huizinga

A magnificent study of life, thought and art in 14th and 15th century France and the Netherlands, long established as a classic.

The Penguin Dictionary of Psychology   Arthur S. Reber

Over 17,000 terms from psychology, psychiatry and related fields are given clear, concise and modern definitions.